The Advanced
90-Minute Resume

The Advanced 90-Minute Resume

Peggy Schmidt

Peterson's Guides

Princeton, New Jersey

Library of Congress Cataloging-in-Publication Data
Schmidt, Peggy J.
    The advanced 90-minute resume / Peggy Schmidt.
      p.   cm.
    ISBN 1-56079-151-9
    1. Resumes (Employment). I. Title. II. Title: Advanced ninety-minute resume.
HF5383.S326 1992
650.14—dc20   91-45722

Composition and design by Peterson's Guides

Printed in the United States of America

10 9 8 7 6 5 4 3 2 1

 Printed on recycled paper

Contents

Acknowledgments

My deepest thanks to those who have contributed their ideas to *The Advanced 90-Minute Resume.*

Lynn Tendler Bignell, principal and cofounder, Gilbert Tweed Associates, New York, New York

Richard J. Chagnon, senior vice president/professional services, Right Associates, Philadelphia, Pennsylvania

Bill Davis, director of marketing, Minotype Typography, Chicago, Illinois

John D. Erdlen, president, Management Dimensions, Inc., and director, Northeast Human Resources Association, Wellesley, Massachusetts

Susan Gordon, president, Lynne Palmer Agency, New York, New York

Virginia Lord, senior vice president/marketing and public relations, Right Associates, Philadelphia, Pennsylvania

Jeanne Miller, public relations coordinator, AlphaGraphics, Tucson, Arizona

Jack Schwartz, area managing director, Source Edp, New York, New York

Barbara Stafford, manager of electronic graphics, AlphaGraphics commercial printing division, Tucson, Arizona

My editors, Jim Gish, Owen O'Donnell, Joy Mastroberardino, and the Peterson's staff

Many thanks to my family—Joe, Ted, and Christina—for their support.

Preface

After my book *Making It on Your First Job: When You're Young, Ambitious, and Inexperienced* came out, relatives and friends—and friends of friends—began asking me to help them put together or revise their resume. The approach I used and refined over time was based on my years of experience and training as a journalist: I asked the job hunter questions in the same way I would if I'd been interviewing him or her for an article. The technique seemed to work no matter who I was helping—my brother, a recent college graduate; a friend who had worked in one profession for ten years but wanted to change careers; my mother, who was going back to work after a twenty-five-year hiatus. "You made me look great!" they told me. They got interviews and they landed good jobs.

I began passing along the highlights of my interview technique to students at the New York University Summer Publishing Institute, where I'm the career coordinator. I've reviewed hundreds of resumes since 1982 and have seen dramatic improvements after students followed my suggestions. Many have told me that they felt much more confident about starting their job search because they knew their resume portrayed them at their best.

I decided to self-publish my "interview approach" to resume writing and offer it to readers of the weekly column I was writing for New York's *Daily News*. Hundreds wrote in to ask for a copy, and some of those called back to say that after following the guide they'd received compliments on their resume from the employers they'd interviewed with.

That prompted me to restudy the resume books on my shelf and the latest releases in bookstores. I found they were thick with sample resumes and jammed with self-assessment exercises, but short on the kind of advice that I considered really helpful. Maybe, I told myself, more people than I'd originally thought could benefit from the interview process.

I expanded and revised the original guide, incorporating the suggestions of readers who had used it. The first trade edition of *The 90-Minute Resume* was published by Peterson's in the spring of 1990.

That book has enjoyed so much success that I created this new volume, *The Advanced 90-Minute Resume,* for job hunters with experience who want to update and revise their current resume. There are special sections devoted to career changers who need to overcome the resistance of potential employers to people who have not followed traditional career paths.

I've refined the interview approach that is the basis of *The 90-Minute Resume* into a new concept called "the coach approach." There's no tougher assignment than sitting down alone with your current resume and trying to figure out how to make it better. But if you have someone who can help you analyze its pluses and minuses and use the interview method to develop new material, you can create a strong marketing piece that can help you land a great job.

I'm the kind of person who would like to play the role of coach with every job hunter who needs help with his or her resume. Since I can't do that, I'm honored that you've decided to have me as the unseen muse who, I hope, will inspire you and your coach to produce a truly outstanding resume.

Peggy Schmidt
April 1992

Preliminaries

How the 90-Minute Process Works

You can revise and strengthen your resume in a relatively short period of time by using the method I've developed from years of teaching resume-writing workshops and working with individuals to perfect their resume. It's called the coach approach.

Few tasks are more daunting than trying to summarize your work life on paper and present it in a way that says, "I'm a terrific candidate. Call me." Figuring out what to highlight and what to discard is at best difficult. But if you enlist the help of another person, someone who has had the experience of writing his or her own resume or of evaluating the resumes of others, your progress will be quicker and the results stronger. Your coach can supply an outsider's perspective, provide feedback on your current resume, and ask questions that will form the basis of your revisions.

If you were to revise your resume on your own, chances are good you would spend hours tinkering with it. The beauty of the 90-minute process is that by following clearly defined steps and using another person—your coach—as a sounding board, interviewer, and resource, you can produce a better product in a much shorter period of time. This book contains all the information the two of you need to produce a resume that will portray you at your best.

Think of your resume as you would a coming attraction for a movie; if the preview is enticing, you're going to want to see the film when it is released. Similarly, a carefully conceived resume can result in a call for an interview. What makes for a winning resume? First, it must be visually inviting—clean and highly readable. Second, it should highlight your experiences and skills in an easy-to-follow format. Third, and perhaps most important, it should point to the results of your efforts, not simply provide job descriptions.

Before you schedule a session with your coach, skim through the book to get an idea of how it works. If your coach has time, a quick read is also the best way for him or her to prepare. If that's not possible, have your coach read the entire "Preliminaries" section and the coach guidelines that are interspersed throughout the book.

An hour and a half is a realistic time period in which to produce a *solid* draft of your resume (producing the final product is discussed in "Design Your Resume" on page 74 and is not included in the 90 minutes).

The 90-minute process consists of six major parts: (1) developing a new job target, (2) critiquing your current resume, (3) using the interview method to add or expand material, (4) translating your notes into resume language, (5) creating a working draft, and (6) perfecting your content.

The time allotted for each part is a general guideline; you may find that you don't need as much or that you need more. The important thing is to take the time you feel you need to successfully complete the step, even if it exceeds the suggested time. Remember, you'll be using your current resume as a starting point—it may already be quite good or it may pale in comparison with its competition. In either case, you can make it into a standout by using this book.

The Advanced 90-Minute Resume is designed to help those who already have some work experience—people who

- Hope to move up in the same field,
- Want to make a lateral move to a related skill area within their field,
- Are hoping to change industries but remain in the same type of job, or
- Plan to change fields.

If you're planning to change fields, some of the steps you'll follow in this book are different from those for people who are in the other categories. "When you are changing direction, it's critical for your resume to communicate what about your background makes your experience a good fit for a new type of job," says Susan Gordon, president of the Lynne Palmer Agency, a personnel agency in New York City that specializes in placing candidates in the book and magazine publishing fields. "If you have analyzed your situation clearly, a potential employer is more likely to see things your way," she adds. To do that in a systematic manner, career changers and their coaches will be given instructions on how to find parallels between past experiences and a new job target and how to translate those similarities into convincing resume language.

One more thing: Believe in yourself. Even if you think that you've done only ordinary things, you are a special person with unique experiences and skills. You can get a better job than you now have or find a job, even if you've been unemployed for weeks or months. Start with the conviction that the resume you'll create is the first step in a new direction. If you follow the steps suggested in *The Advanced 90-Minute Resume,* the process of creating your resume will help you focus your job objective and organize your experiences. Knowing where you're going and how your past jobs have prepared you to take that next step is critical to convincing an employer that you are the right candidate. Clearly expressing your ambition and accomplishments on paper will give you confidence and direction as you begin your job search.

If you are changing careers, read the following section. If not, skip ahead to "Selecting the Right Coach" on page 8.

Advance Work for Career Changers

Changing careers isn't something that can be done lightly or easily, which is why you have more advance work to do before revising your resume than do job hunters hoping to move up in the same field, change industries, or make a lateral move within an industry.

Deciding to look for a job in a new field requires a lot of soul searching and researching—soul searching because you may have to forego status and perks (not to mention income) when you make the leap to a new career and researching because you can't make a well-informed judgment about your move without it.

It's critical to develop a resume that reflects your carefully thought-through decision, and this book will help you do just that. Your current resume is a summary of what you've already done, not what you hope to do, which is why it's important to do the following before overhauling it.

- Conduct an analysis of your skills, interests, and talents to determine your ideal job.

- Read everything you can about the field and type of job(s) you've pinpointed.

- Talk to a variety of people who work in the field about their experiences.

- Identify the hurdles breaking into a new field will present.

- Weigh the pros and cons of making such a change.

- Complete educational or licensing requirements (or be in the process of doing so).

If you need suggestions on how to begin this process, turn to "Career Decision Resources" on page 95.

Another fact to keep in mind: The higher the unemployment rate, the more difficult it is to convince an employer to hire a career changer over someone who has been working steadily in the field and accumulating expertise. On the other hand, when the number of exceptional candidates for any one job is low, an employer is more willing to risk hiring someone whose experience varies widely from what's expected. Says John D. Erdlen, president of Management Dimensions, Inc., a consulting firm in Wellesley, Massachusetts, and executive director of the Northeast Regional Human Resources Association: "What can make all the difference in the world is a guardian angel—a mentor type—who is willing to vouch for you and say, 'She's worth the risk.'"

The risk, as many employers see it, is that the career changer may take longer to get up to speed or be less tuned into the nuances of the job than the person who has followed a more traditional career path. An even bigger concern is that the career changer won't be able to perform as well in the job as someone who is not changing careers. That's why having someone such as a former boss, who knows your work habits and capabilities, provide reassurance to a potential employer is a big plus. Nevertheless, before your mentor is called in or if you don't have one, you'll have to make your own case for why you should seriously be considered as a candidate. If your first introduction to an employer is your resume, it's essential for it to communicate that

- You have done your research and understand what the position requires,

- You are serious about making the change, and

- You would be a great candidate for the job.

Your coach can play an important support role in helping you accomplish that. Ideally, he or she is someone who currently works in or who has had experience in the field you hope to switch to. The advantage of such a coach is that he or she knows the jargon, has a handle on the thinking of people in that profession, and can make suggestions you can rely on. If you can't enlist the help of such a person, don't worry—an intelligent and thoughtful person who has the characteristics discussed in the next section will be fine.

7

Selecting the Right Coach

Now that you have an overview of where you're going, you can begin your first assignment—identify the right person to help you. The ideal coach is someone who is familiar with your field and has at least as much, if not more, experience in it as you. He or she may be a colleague (who can be trusted to keep a confidence), a former colleague, someone you know through a professional organization, a former client, or a classmate. The coach should have good oral and written communication skills. After all, his or her job is to recognize weak points on your resume and suggest how they can be strengthened. As an interviewer, his or her ability to elicit information from you is critical.

If there's no one who readily fits the bill, a good bet is any experienced professional whose judgment you respect. That person might be a relative, neighbor, or someone you know through community or church activities. Your spouse or the person with whom you are romantically involved may be the most convenient person to recruit as coach, but keep in mind that he or she will probably not be as objective in his or her critique or suggestions as someone less involved in your life.

Most important, your coach must take the responsibility seriously and be willing to spend 90 minutes to ask good questions and give you thoughtful feedback.

A Crash Course for Coaches

As coach, you are about to play an enjoyable and important role in this unique resume creation process. Just what is expected of you? Three things:

1. Critique the job hunter's current resume. Your perspective will be invaluable because you can more easily flag information gaps, unclear lan-

guage, and organizational problems, among other things.

2. Interview the job hunter. Your questions to the job hunter (lists are provided) make the process of getting information down on paper an easy one.

3. Provide feedback and ideas. As you work with the job hunter in choosing words to communicate his or her background and organizing the information in a way that can be easily followed, you can act as a sounding board and suggest ways of doing things that may not have otherwise occurred to him or her.

You will find the role of coach easy if you've had experience evaluating resumes as an employer or if you have experience in the field the job hunter hopes to find his or her next job in. If you have neither, rest assured that your good judgment and keen eye will be invaluable in this 90-minute process.

As you offer comments or ask questions, remember:

Be encouraging and phrase your comments in a positive way. Many people feel uncomfortable talking about themselves and their accomplishments, so be sure to put the job hunter at ease by being a good listener and complimenting his or her answers. Likewise, being constructive in your criticisms will create a better working relationship.

Don't hesitate to probe. If you don't understand something the job hunter has said or written, ask for an explanation. Why? Because if the same words make their way into the final version of the resume, the employer who reads the resume is likely to be confused too.

Make sure the job hunter doesn't sell himself short. Job hunters often provide too little information. Your job is to ask questions that will draw out specifics, particularly numbers that will give a job task or an accomplishment a context in which to be better understood.

Coach guidelines are interspersed throughout the book to assist you. Be sure to read them before you begin the work described in the corresponding sections. The role you're about to play in helping the job hunter is an important one. Good luck!

Are You an Expert Resume Reviewer?

You may have had experience evaluating the resumes of prospective job candidates for a position in your company. You may have a keen eye for spotting people with the right background, but are you aware of the other factors that may consciously or subconsciously affect your decisions?

Before you and your coach begin working on your new resume, the two of you should take this quiz to find out how good you are at pinpointing resume mistakes big and small. The more aware you are of the things that weaken a resume, the less likely you are to make those same errors on your own resume.

On a separate piece of paper, identify words, phrases, graphic elements, or sections that you feel are inconsistent, unclear, disorganized, or inconclusive in the resume that appears on the next page. Jot down brief explanations for your choices. There are ten mistakes and two major omissions.

Resume of

Christina S. Edwards

222 Woodson Avenue
Liberty, Ohio 44071

Work: (419) 555-7145
Home: (419) 555-6342

EDUCATION

B.A., Marketing, Miami University, Oxford, Ohio, 1979
Specialized Training—15 sales and marketing courses sponsored by my
employer and professional association, 1984–1991

EXPERIENCE

Position: Coordinator, Worldwide Marketing and Advertising
Company: Data Information, Inc.
Location: Toledo, Ohio (419) 555-6000
Reported to: Robert Elswood, Vice President, Marketing
Dates: 9/89–present

Responsibilities: Coordinate worldwide promotions and associated marketing programs designed to stimulate usage of database network. Obtain data from user members and regions to track and report results of worldwide promotions. Interface with promotion, advertising, and public relations agencies and consultants.

Position: Assistant to Vice President of International Marketing
Company: Data Information, Inc.
Location: Toledo, Ohio (419) 555-6000
Reported to: Jane Melbourne, Vice President, International Marketing
Dates: 6/87–9/89

Responsibilities: Aided and assisted the vice president in development and implementation of international promotions. Researched and prepared external communications including memos, slide presentations, and brochures. Tracked and monitored all budget expenditures for compliance and variance analysis.

Position: Marketing Representative
Company: Research Software Ventures
Location: Cincinnati, Ohio (419) 555-1100
Reported to: Michael Casa, Marketing Manager
Dates: 1/84–5/87

Responsibilities: Developed and serviced fifty clients. Wrote and produced sales presentations. Promoted from secretary to marketing rep within six months.

Prior to 1984, I worked as the administrator of a family business, a nursing home, which was sold in 1983.

Personal Interests: Sports, travel, music.

Let's see how well you fared. The errors are categorized as content, organization, and design mistakes. Some are much more flagrant than others, but even those that seem trivial can make a resume look less professional.

Content

1. The single biggest weakness of this resume is in the Experience section. Christina's responsibilities come across like job descriptions written by a personnel department—the language is dry and impersonal. Two major sins of omission occur here, too: Christina has not mentioned one accomplishment, and she doesn't use numbers to quantify the scope of her responsibilities.

2. Another content shortfall is the way in which Christina treated her first job experience— "Prior to 1984." Perhaps because she felt that it was not related to marketing, she used only one line to describe four years of experience. Since she was in a very responsible position and developed skills that may be a factor in the next job she is considered for, she should have given it more weight by setting up that job the same way she did her more recent jobs and by highlighting a few achievements or tasks.

3. "Resume of" is not necessary. The format of the information tells the reader that this is a resume.

4. The personal interests are so general that they contribute nothing to her profile. In addition, this heading doesn't match the two other major section headings, which is a design problem.

Organization

1. The Education section is misplaced. Job hunters who are not recent graduates should almost al-

ways lead off with Experience. An exception would be the resume of a career changer who has just completed an academic program that is a prerequisite to the field he or she hopes to enter.

2. "Specialized Training" should precede the college entry under Education because it's more recent. If a job hunter has taken courses that prepared him or her for the job he or she is trying to win, it should be mentioned by name. Resist the temptation to highlight information or a heading that appears only once as Christina did by using asterisks before and after Specialized Training.

Design

1. The headings Position, Employer, Location, Reported to, Dates, and Responsibilities not only clutter up the resume but also present the content ineffectively. The "Reported to" headings and categories and the phone numbers listed on the "Location" lines can be deleted; they belong on a separate sheet listing references.

2. The Responsibilities sections are difficult to read because they are blocks of copy. It would be more graphically pleasing if Christina had indented each responsibility or used bullets or another graphic element to separate the items.

3. Christina's name is in a disproportionately large point size. It should be at the most two point sizes larger than the rest of the type.

4. "Experience" is not underlined. The graphic elements used to distinguish each heading should be consistent.

A round of applause if you caught the majority of these mistakes—you have a keen eye for resume strengths and weaknesses. But don't worry too much if some of these errors eluded you. Each of the mistakes described here will be explained in greater detail in the pages ahead.

As you can see on the next page, after using the process described in this book, Christina was able to create a much more descriptive and convincing resume.

CHRISTINA S. EDWARDS

222 Woodson Avenue   Work: (419) 555-7145
Liberty, Ohio 44071   Home: (419) 555-6342

WORK EXPERIENCE

Data Information, Inc., Toledo, Ohio—June 1987–present

Coordinator, Worldwide Marketing and Advertising, September 1989–present
- Coordinate five worldwide promotions and associated marketing programs that have increased usage of database network 20 percent since January 1990
- Designed system to obtain data from user members and regions to track and report amount of usage; information has become instrumental in developing new sales strategies
- Proposed tripling advertising budget; plan accepted by senior management (March 1990), which helped boost database into top three services nationwide (June 1991)

Assistant to Vice President of International Marketing, June 1987–August 1989
- Assisted in development and implementation of three international promotions
- Researched and prepared copy and visuals for twenty multimedia presentations and ten sales brochures; twice received letters of commendation from director of sales for these efforts
- Tracked and monitored department budget expenditures of $500,000 after one year on job because "she is a financial whiz and a person of great integrity" (job performance report)

Research Software Ventures, Cincinnati, Ohio—January 1984–May 1987

Marketing Representative
- Expanded list of clients from thirty to fifty in one year
- Wrote and produced sales presentations, which management decided to have all reps use because of their effectiveness
- Promoted from secretary to marketing rep within six months

Golden Acres Nursing Home, Toledo, Ohio—September 1979–November 1983

Administrator
- Assumed operating responsibility for this 100-bed facility (a family-owned business) after having worked in various part-time and summer positions there for eight years
- Supervised construction of building addition (adding twenty beds) and modernizing kitchen and bathrooms
- Added two professional positions to existing three, upgrading therapy and recreational services to patients; received commendation from State Supervisory Board

EDUCATION

Professional training: Fifteen sales and marketing courses sponsored by my employer and professional association, 1984–91

B.A., Marketing, Miami University, Oxford, Ohio, 1979

INTERESTS

Marathon running (have completed ten marathons in five countries), listening to and collecting 1940s big band jazz

Revising Your Resume

Before You Start

Before you sit down with your coach, it's a good idea to gather the materials you'll need to work with and to prepare a few things to facilitate your time together.

Tools of the Trade

You'll need the following items for the 90-minute process.

- Several pens or pencils.
- At least ten blank sheets of paper (lined or unlined).
- Two copies of your current resume.
- One photocopy of the Work Experience Evaluation Checklist on page 27 and the Copy Checklist on page 70 (recommended)
- A typewriter or computer (recommended)

First, Your Fact Sheets

Your current resume probably doesn't reflect the job you now hold, and, if it's been some time since you revised it, it may not include other jobs you've held. Your coach will be interviewing you about what you did and accomplished on those jobs. By preparing in advance what I call fact sheets, you can help your coach phrase questions and move through the interview more quickly.

Use a blank sheet of paper for each job you need to add. Across the top of each sheet, write

- Your job title,
- Your employer's name and location (city and state), and
- Your dates of employment (month and year).

Next, write down three or four main responsibilities and/or accomplishments for each job. Don't worry about the wording. What's important is to provide enough information for your coach to ask you about them in detail. Once you're done, set these fact sheets aside. They'll be used in "Interviewing for Information," which begins on page 28.

Your Job Target

The second step is to write down your job target—describe the position you'd like to land. The more focused you are about what you want to do and the more knowledgeable you are about the responsibilities of that job and the skills required, the easier it will be to develop a resume that will attract the attention of employers you want to work for.

"We urge all of our clients to start revising their resume by coming up with a job objective," says Richard J. Chagnon, a senior vice president of Right Associates, a worldwide outplacement firm headquartered in Philadelphia. "The reason? It forces you to think not only in terms of what you have done but what you can do," he says.

Whether or not you intend to use a job objective on your resume, you should write one for you and your coach to use as a basis for making decisions about which skills and experience to emphasize. Name a specific job in a particular industry; the more specific and realistic your target, the easier it will be to decide which jobs, responsibilities, and accomplishments to highlight. Don't worry about expressing your job target in resume language for now, since the immediate purpose is to help you make decisions about content. (The issue of whether it's advisable to include a job objective will be discussed in "Create a Working Draft," which begins on page 50.)

EXAMPLE

Job Objective

I'd like to work as an international tax specialist in a position that would involve making recommendations on strategic planning issues and helping senior managers make financial policy decisions.

The details of this job description—in particular, the person's interest in international taxation, strategic planning, and decision making—can be very helpful in highlighting those aspects of his or her experience and skills.

Next, based on what you know about your target job, write down four or five tasks that someone in that position would be responsible for. Doing this will enable you to make better judgments about which tasks and accomplishments from past jobs to emphasize on your new resume.

EXAMPLE

What I'd like to do next:

> Work in a corporate office environment as an industrial hygienist

Job tasks of new job target:

- Investigate the adequacy of ventilation, lighting, or other work conditions that may affect employee health or safety.
- Collect samples of dust or other toxic materials for analysis.
- Educate employees about on-the-job health hazards and preventive measures.
- Review processes that result in employee exposure to noise, chemicals, or biological hazards.
- Write detailed reports of findings and recommendations in a clear, concise, persuasive manner.

The third step is to identify the two, three, or four areas of expertise under which these job tasks would fit. In the example on the preceding page, those areas are investigation, education, and communication. The benefit of this particular exercise is that it provides a basis for you and your coach to analyze how your past experiences mesh with your job target.

If you've never before thought about how to group like sets of skills under a large heading, the following chart can help you. It doesn't contain every area of expertise—that list would include hundreds of entries. But by looking over the action verbs listed under each area, you'll get a better idea of how skills can be organized. (Areas of expertise are sometimes referred to as functions or functional areas and are used as the main section headings in functional resumes—resumes organized by area of expertise.)

Areas of Expertise

Accounting	Administration	Advertising	Coaching
Analyze	Administer	Conceptualize	Coordinate
Audit	Control	Create	Direct
Calculate	Direct	Design	Instruct
Estimate	Institute	Develop	Lead
Examine	Manage	Formulate	Motivate
Plan	Organize	Negotiate	Organize
Project	Oversee	Plan	Schedule
Review	Program	Write	Train

Communications	Design	Finance	Fund-Raising
Conceptualize	Conceptualize	Analyze	Address
Develop	Create	Calculate	Contact
Edit	Develop	Compile	Develop
Interview	Illustrate	Diagnose	Propose
Outline	Lay out	Formulate	Raise
Present	Render	Leverage	Solicit
Research		Negotiate	Write
Write		Research	

Management	Personnel	Public Relations	Research
Administer	Administer	Develop	Analyze
Analyze	Analyze	Market	Calculate
Conduct	Evaluate	Promote	Determine
Control	Interview	Represent	Investigate
Direct	Provide	Research	Solve
Implement	Screen	Speak	Study
Supervise	Test	Write	Test

Undecided About What's Next? Try the Balance Sheet Approach

If you aren't sure what your next best career step is, you should research your options. There are many ways to do that, among them talking to people in your field whose judgment you trust, taking a short course in making career decisions, or going the self-help route with a career decision-making book such as Richard Nelson Bolles' *What Color Is Your Parachute?*

If you can't decide from among your options, try the balance sheet approach to making a decision. The concept is easy. You rate the things about a job that are most important to you and give each factor a numerical value. By adding up the score, you can determine which option has the highest rating. Start by making a list of all the possibilities you are entertaining. Then, beginning with the first one on your list, assign a weight (on a scale of one to five, five being the best) to the factors that influence each job's appeal. These include expected salary, job level, ability to work independently, security, variety of job tasks, potential for recognition, work schedule, hours, and any other factors important to you. Add up the points for each one and compare the totals. The job or jobs that get the highest points are the best bets for your next position.

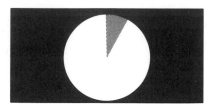

Time for this exercise: 5 minutes

Is Your Job Target on Target?

With the advance work done, it's now time to call in your coach and start the clock. The first part of the 90-minute process the two of you will tackle is evaluating your job target. In the sections that follow you will evaluate your current resume to get an idea of what changes need to be made to present your background in the most favorable light and undertake the interview.

In evaluating your targeted job, be open to your coach's comments and suggestions. He or she may bring up points that haven't occurred to you and that may be convincing reasons why you might want to alter it—or add others. Having more than one job target isn't a problem, but you may want to consider creating several editions of your resume, each geared to a specific target. (This can be easily accomplished if you are creating your resume with word processing or desktop publishing software.)

Coach Guideline: Evaluate the job target. Is it clearly stated? Is it too narrow? Too broad? Does it make sense given the person's current or previous job? Are the tasks and areas of expertise of the job target analyzed correctly? You may not be able to judge this accurately unless you have more experience in the target field than the job hunter.

Ready? Start the clock. You have 5 minutes.

If you are a career changer, after completing this exer-cize skip ahead to "For Career Changers Only: The Match-ing Game" on page 32; if you're not, continue on to the next page.

Time for this exercise: Total time elapsed:
35 minutes   40 minutes

The Jewel of Your Resume

Now you and your coach will evaluate the most critical section of your resume—the Work Experience section. "I think it's very important to be able to see a thread of connection from one job to another," says Lynn Tendler Bignell, principal and cofounder of Gilbert Tweed Associates, an international search firm headquartered in New York City. "If I can see the connection among customers, the type of product, their territory, marketing experience, or whatever, I get the sense that the person controlled his or her career rather than the other way around," she says, "and that's an important factor in my selecting one candidate over another."

Critiquing the Work Experience section can give both of you ideas about what to focus on during the interview. One of you can use the photocopy of the Work Experience Evaluation Checklist you have made and the other can read it on the following page. The two of you should scan the list, but first your coach should take a few minutes to read over your current resume.

Using the questions as a guideline, assess your resume job by job. There are two forums for discussing your reactions: (1) Go through it together question by question, take turns offering your views, and write down your points of agreement; and (2) jot down your comments separately

26

about each question and then compare notes. Your coach may pick up on things that you cannot see because you created the resume. By the two of you discussing the weaknesses of your current resume as you each see them, you'll be able to better focus your efforts during the interview and writing portion of the 90-minute process.

Work Experience Evaluation Checklist

1. Are there a sufficient number of responsibilities under each job?
2. Do the responsibilities provide enough detail about your skills and expertise?
3. Are there enough tasks listed that support your new job target, or should more be added?
4. Is the language of the descriptions clear and concise, and does each begin with a strong action verb?
5. Are there numbers and percentages that quantify the scope of your responsibilities?
6. Is there too much repetition of job tasks or action verbs?
7. Are there examples or evidence to back up claims?
8. Have you included descriptions of accomplishments in each job?
9. Are there numbers, percentages, or details to quantify accomplishments?
10. Are dates of employment given for each job listed?

If you've chosen to go through the checklist separately, either one of you can start the discussion, although your coach may feel more comfortable if you go first. The easiest way to proceed is to work down the resume job by job. Make it a give-and-take conversation with both of you addressing the same question, rather than each of you running through your list, so that you cover the same ground together. You may find that if a weakness exists, such as not including any numbers or accomplishments, it may well occur throughout an entire section.

Your goal in this exercise is to identify what needs the most work. It may be the case that a series of jobs you had with your current employer need consolidating to eliminate repetition or that you need to work at developing the connections among your jobs so that you'll come across as someone who controlled his or her career.

Coach Guideline: Avoid getting bogged down over a small point—if necessary, set it aside for later consideration. As you talk about specific points, keep these questions in mind. (1) Are job experiences presented in a logical and easy-to-follow way? (2) Do they support the kind of position the job hunter is going after? (3) Are the connections among jobs clear—are there links between skills, areas of expertise, or industries?

Put aside the book now, and begin the exercise. You have 15 minutes.

Interviewing for Information

The point of having your coach ask questions is to get you to talk about your work experience, which, for most people, is easier than writing about it. No matter how good you think your Work Experience section is, explaining your job history in a conversation will probably help you improve what you have on your current resume and fact sheets.

It's the coach's job to ask, "Explain what you mean," or "Can you give me an example?" if he or she doesn't understand your answer. Try to use words that clearly and simply describe your job responsibilities, skills, and accomplishments. Avoid using jargon and technical terms. And, at this stage, don't talk in resume language—try to make your answers concrete and descriptive.

Both you and your coach should keep a pen or pencil in hand as you conduct the interview. You'll want to jot down words, phrases, and well-expressed ideas as soon as you have answered a question to your interviewer's satisfaction. The coach can help by noting key words and phrases as you speak. Before moving on to the next question, read back what you've got. Work together to get down a phrase that contains an action verb (what you did), a direct object (thing), and qualifying clauses (details about what you did).

EXAMPLE

Organized --- committee --- to evaluate laboratory procedures.

If you have a tape recorder, you may want to tape the session. It will allow you to rewind and play back parts of the Q and A, which is particularly helpful if something brilliant is said and promptly forgotten.

Coach Guideline: You should have the job hunter's fact sheets in front of you. Start with the most recently held job and work backward. If the job hunter has already given some thought to what he or she does on the job and what his or her accomplishments have been, you may not need to go beyond the first two questions for each job. The additional questions are suggestions for what to ask if you need to dig deeper. It's crucial to get numbers whenever possible and at least one or two accomplishments or results for each job. Remember to spend more time on those positions that relate to the job target.

Finally, keep the interview on track. Don't let the job hunter stray from the question you have asked—simply say, "That's good information, but I'm not sure it's necessary here."

- What exactly did you do on your job on a regular (daily, weekly, or monthly) basis? Start with the tasks you consider most important and try to come up with at least five, even if you don't include all of them in your final resume.
- Did any of your accomplishments ever result in a promotion, raise, or other type of recognition? Please describe them and quantify with num-

bers, for example, a *10 percent* bonus or a *doubling* of your client list.

- Did you manage the work of one or more employees? If so, how many? At what level (clerical, technical, senior staff, etc.) were those employees?

- What are some of the most important projects you worked on? Briefly describe their purpose and your role. Did you meet or exceed the expectations of your boss (or management)?

- Did you suggest an idea that was successfully implemented by your boss, department, or company? Please describe what it involved, your role in making it work, and any credit or compliments you received as a result.

- Did you train one or more employees to do something you know how to do well? Describe the nature of the task or tasks, whether you did it on your own initiative, and whether others learned how to do it successfully.

- What have you done that has made you feel satisfied or won praise from your boss, management, or clients?

• • • •

SAMPLE CONVERSATION

Situation: A job hunter who is currently director of development at a small liberal arts college hopes to land a job with the same title at a much larger private university.

Coach: What do you do as a director of development?

Job Hunter: I have four major areas of responsibility: coming up with fresh ideas for fundraising campaigns, maintaining good relationships with benefactors, identifying

	new potential donors, and managing a staff of five who implement fund-raising activities.
Coach:	How do you maintain good relationships?
Job Hunter:	I write personal letters, make phone calls, produce a newsletter, and stop by to see people in their homes or offices.
Coach:	How does this job differ from your previous one as a development specialist?
Job Hunter:	My main responsibilities as a specialist were implementing other people's ideas, and I managed one clerical member of the staff.
Coach:	What kind of results have you had in your current job?
Job Hunter:	I created a successful annual fund-raising campaign that we have used for four years. The first year, it increased donations by 10 percent, and that has steadily increased by an average of five percent each year since. Our benefactor base has increased by one third.
Coach:	Are there any less tangible accomplishments you can claim credit for?
Job Hunter:	I introduced incentive plans for the entire staff. Morale is better and turnover is down.

What to write down:

—Generating new fund-raising ideas
  • Result: new annual fund-raising campaign—10 percent increase first year, about 5 percent growth each year for the last three years
—Maintaining relationships with benefactors
  • Writing personal letters, making phone calls, producing a newsletter, making in-person visits

> —Identifying new potential donors
> —Managing a staff of five
>> • Result: improved morale, reduced turnover

This sample conversation is a sliver of how an actual interview or conversation might go. The coach could, for example, ask the job hunter to expand on each of his or her four main areas of responsibilities to get additional details. The coach might also probe for additional results. The question about how the current and previous jobs differed can help you decide how to handle unnecessary repetition of job tasks.

Now that you know the basics of doing a good interview, it's time to start asking questions. When you've completed this exercise, page ahead to "Coming Up with Great Resume Language" on page 39.

Time for this
exercise:
35 minutes

Total time
elapsed:
40 minutes

For Career Changers Only: The Matching Game

If you're looking for a job in a new field because you no longer feel challenged or excited about your work or because your field is retrenching, it's important to carefully think through your approach to finding your next position. The biggest hurdle you must overcome is convincing a potential employer that you are qualified for the job. "The resume writer has to come up with what I call 'instant recognition factors' so that the reader will say, 'It wouldn't hurt to talk to her even though her background is out of the ordinary,'" says Management Dimensions' Erdlen.

What are instant recognition factors? They are skills and experiences that are gained in one context (usually a job but also through course work, in an avocation or hobby, or from community or professional activities) but that could be effectively used in another context. These factors are also called transferable skills and experiences.

Scan your current resume to identify your own transferable skills. Some may jump out at you because the action verbs you used to describe job tasks may be the same as or similar to those required in the new career you have targeted. You and your coach should each work with separate copies of your current resume and fact sheets. Put check marks next to the job responsibilities and accomplishments that may be evidence of your qualification to do the work that's the core of your new job target.

Coach Guideline: *Ask the following questions for any task that supports the job hunter's case for making a change to his or her new career but needs expanding (one that has been checked by the job hunter or you). Be sure to include job tasks from positions listed on the fact sheets as well as from the current resume.*

Questions

- Can you explain with more details what this job task involved?
- What skills were involved in executing this task?
- What role did this task play in accomplishing your work objectives?

• • • •

SAMPLE CONVERSATION

Situation: A high school English teacher who hopes to get a job as an instructor in the training and development department of a corporation.

Job task on current resume:

- Prepared lesson plans for literature and writing classes for thirty high school seniors

Coach: Tell me more about what was involved in preparing lesson plans.

Job Hunter: I developed outlines for what I would cover in class by working with the history, social studies, and art teachers so that there were links between what each of us was teaching. I tried to come up with interesting ideas for homework assignments that would involve reading and writing skills. I even published the best ones in a weekly newspaper.

Coach: What skills did you use in preparing lesson plans?

Job Hunter: I suppose it involved analytical skills because it was an interdisciplinary exercise. It involved teamwork—an ability to work with others. It required imagination and creativity and a practical sense of what would motivate students to work.

Coach: What role did lesson preparation play in your overall teaching responsibilities?

Job Hunter: A critical one. Without good planning, I wouldn't have been able to present my own thoughts in a cohesive way. Nor would the students have sensed an order or structure to what they were learning. And that would have affected how attentive they were—and how much they participated in class and in doing their homework assignments.

What to write down:
— Develop lesson outlines
— Come up with interesting ideas for homework assignments
— Published best papers in newspaper
— Involved analytical skills and teamwork—imagination and creativity

—Knowing what would motivate students, keep their attention, and affect participation

Now, start the interview. You have 20 minutes to complete it.

Identifying Skills and Experiences Outside of a Job Context

In addition to finding parallels in past job experiences for your impending career change, you may also find evidence to support your claims by looking at your involvements beyond your job. They too can help make a case for being a candidate worth considering.

Coach Guideline: *Use the action verbs from the description of the tasks of the targeted job and ask the following questions. If you see a possible connection between an activity that is mentioned on the current resume and a task from the job hunter's ideal job, ask about it in particular.*

Questions

- Did you ever have to [insert action verb] in a job, volunteer experience, avocation, or hobby?
- Under what circumstances did you do it?
- What skills did your activity involve?
- How often did you do this task?
- Can you point to anything positive that resulted from your efforts?

• • • •

SAMPLE CONVERSATION

Situation: A recruiter who works for a college hopes to get a position as an account executive with a public relations firm.

First action verb: Research.

Coach: Have you ever conducted research?

Job Hunter: I am familiar with researching issues because I worked as a volunteer with the World Wildlife Federation.

Coach: Under what circumstances did you do research?

Job Hunter: I was an active member of our group's Scientists' Liaison committee. I did scientific literature reviews to find scientists whose work had an impact on the wildlife issues we were promoting. I would then speak to the author of the study and contact others he or she suggested to get even more information.

Coach: What skills were involved in doing this research?

Job Hunter: Familiarity with how reference books are organized, for one. Also, the ability to come up with key words to start the information search. My knowledge of how computer databases work came in handy, too, since I sometimes looked for information that way.

Coach: How often did you do this kind of research?

Job Hunter: About 10 hours every month.

Coach: Can you point to any results of your research work?

Job Hunter: Definitely. I have already been involved in the research of four major projects. After being accepted by the committee head and the scientific consultant our organization retains, my research was used to define causes we supported and was cited in four separate campaigns, one of which was credited with being pivotal in raising $1-million to help save rain forests in Guyana.

What to write down:

—Researched issues as World Wildlife Federation volunteer

—Reviewed literature and interviewed scientists who did studies

—Familiarity with reference books—able to conduct key word searches manually or on computer

—Did 10 hours of research monthly for last year

—Work accepted by committee head and scientific consultant and used in four separate campaigns— one credited with being pivotal in raising $1-million to help save rain forests in Guyana.

Ready, set, start asking questions! You have 15 minutes.

Translate Transferable Skills into Easily Understood Language

Now it's time to go over the interview notes and decide how to phrase your experiences on your revised resume. Again, it's important to write about the transferable skills and tasks in a way that will be readily understood by an employer in your targeted field.

Start writing on a clean sheet of paper. (If you have access to a typewriter or computer, using it will make this step go even faster.) On the left side, write the heading "Transferable Experience" and copy your interview notes underneath it, one entry per line. Each entry should consist of an action verb plus a noun and, perhaps, a qualifying phrase. On the right side of the page write the heading "Resume Copy."

For instance, if the high school teacher presented in the sample conversation on page 33 completed this exercise, her sheet would look like this:

Transferable Experience	Resume Copy
Developed lesson plans	Developed course outline
Came up with interesting assignments	Designed innovative learning tasks
Published best papers in newspaper	Well versed in using motivational tools

You and your coach should go down your list item by item and brainstorm for better ways to phrase each in light of your new job target. A thesaurus or a book that talks about processes in the job field can be helpful. The bottom line is to come up with language that will make it easy for the resume reader to see that you not only understand what the job tasks of your new career choices are but that you have already done them in another context.

Before you start this exercise read through "Coming Up with Great Resume Language," which begins on the next page.

Time for this exercise: Total time elapsed:
15 minutes   55 minutes

Coming Up with Great Resume Language

Your next task is to consolidate the responsibilities and accomplishments of each job into concise statements. But before you start the clock, read through this section.

As you begin this exercise, don't feel restricted to using the words you have in your notes—it's very likely those descriptions will be too long. In editing the entries on your fact sheets, search for words that will link thoughts or more clearly convey the tasks. Begin each statement with an action verb and use the past tense for all except your current job. Avoid making the verb a noun (i.e., using "negotiation skills" instead of "negotiate"). Don't end verbs with "ing."

You may find the task of condensing your interview notes into the highly specific shorthand language of a resume daunting—even if you frequently write as part of your current job. Try using one of these easy-to-follow formulas.

Formula 1

(A) Action verb (present tense for a current job, past tense for a previously held job) *plus*

(B) Object or people *plus*

(C) To or for whom; of, on, or from what; by, through, or with what

EXAMPLES

Promoted --- pet products and accessories --- at trade shows

Designed --- corporate retirement plans --- for client companies

Analyzed --- effectiveness --- of inventory system

Formula 2

(A) Compound action verbs *plus*

(B) Object quantified and/or described *plus*

(C) To or for whom; of, on, or from what; by, through, or with what *plus*

(D) Descriptor

EXAMPLES

Created and implemented --- dBase IV mailing label programs --- for direct-mail catalog operation --- of client firms

Demonstrated --- new customer services --- to sales representatives --- on a weekly basis

Negotiated --- contracts --- with equipment maintenance managers --- in ten foreign countries

Don't feel confined by these formulas; they are merely guidelines for getting your word across clearly and simply. If you need ideas for action verbs, consult the chart on the next page. It contains synonyms for ten action verbs that describe job tasks. For more help in coming up with descriptive action verbs, consult a thesaurus.

Calculate	Care for	Coordinate	Decide
Analyze	Administer to	Arrange	Determine
Compute	Attend to	Assign	Evaluate
Estimate	Look after	Organize	Judge
Figure	Serve	Regulate	Select
Take account of	Watch over	Systematize	Weigh
Manage	**Market**	**Mediate**	**Route**
Administer	Deal in	Accommodate	Direct
Head	Sell	Bring to terms	Expedite
Lead	Shop	Pacify	Guide
Oversee		Reconcile	Schedule
Supervise		Settle	Track
Train	**Write**		
Coach	Communicate		
Inform	Compile		
Instruct	Compose		
Teach	Draft		
Tutor			

EXAMPLES

What you have written on your work experience fact sheet:

In charge of nursing care unit annual report—involves tallying patient counts and turnover and selecting comments from surveys of patients and families and written feedback from doctors and other professional personnel. (31 words)

How to translate it on your resume:

- Produce nursing care unit annual report featuring patient information and feedback from patients, their families, and doctors and other staff professionals. (20 words)

What you have written on your work experience fact sheet:

Make sure patients are matched to nurses most familiar with their medical condition and monitor progress of

nurse/patient teams on a daily basis to ensure best possible care. (28 words)

How to translate it on your resume:
- Maintain quality patient care by delegating appropriate patient-care assignments and moni-
  toring nurse/patient relationships. (15 words)

If you're using a computer and your word processing
program has a word counting feature, get quick counts of
how long your revised job descriptions and accomplishments are by keyboarding the text now.

Time for this exercise: Total time elapsed:
5 minutes   60 minutes

What Are You an Expert At?

At this point you have drafted new copy for your resume. It's time to analyze your collection of job tasks and accomplishments to identify your areas of expertise.

Why is this important? "Forcing yourself to think about your background in categories of skills, experience, and knowledge helps you mentally organize your thoughts for an interview and is particularly good preparation for answering that often-asked question, 'Tell me about yourself,'" says Right Associates' Chagnon. Furthermore, it's a good way to get a handle on which items should be emphasized. You have already identified the areas of expertise required for your new job target. The tasks and accomplishments that belong with those headings should be the first ones mentioned under each job entry.

Finally, because you are constructing the skeleton of a functional resume in this exercise, you'll be able to decide whether that format is preferable to a chronological one (the format that lists positions in chronological order beginning with the most recent). "The Format Issue," which begins on page 46, discusses formats in greater detail.

For this exercise, you and your coach should make a list of the action verbs and the key nouns that begin each task or accomplishment you've written down. Next, decide which of the three or four areas of expertise needed for your targeted job each belongs under. (Refer back to step three in "First, Your Fact Sheets" on page 19.)

EXAMPLE

Situation: The following are descriptions of the job tasks and accomplishments of an operations director whose current job is with a major retailer. His next job target is to become relocation director for a major corporation that has satellite divisions. The identified areas of expertise for the targeted job are contract negotiation, financial planning, and communication. Because the first two items on his list, however, didn't fit under any of those headings, this job hunter and his coach consulted the chart on page 22 and decided that management and administration were the appropriate headings for those tasks and others that followed.

Supervise operations managers— *Management*

Direct training programs— *Administration*

Plan budgets— *Financial planning*

Reduced expenditures— *Financial planning*

Present recommendations to management— *Communication*

Negotiate contracts— *Contract negotiation*

Supervise contractor performance— *Management*

Manage facility openings/closings— *Management*

Produce systems manuals— *Communication*

Provide support services— *Administration*

Negotiate services of subcontractors— *Contract negotiation*

Prepare/submit bids— *Contract negotiation*

On his new resume, this job hunter should highlight the tasks or accomplishments that were marked communication, financial planning, or contract negotiation. In a chronological resume, that can be done by positioning those tasks or accomplishments in the first and second bullets under each job. Why do this? Because the resume reader is more likely to read those. If they're interesting, the reader will pay more attention to the ones that follow. If they're not, he or she may skip the others.

If this job hunter was constructing a functional resume, the section headings would be the areas of expertise—communication, financial planning, and contract negotiation.

Again, the clearer you make the connection between your skills and accomplishments and the areas of expertise in the targeted job, the easier it will be for an employer to recognize that you are a viable candidate.

The Format Issue

A chronological resume is still the preferred format and with good reason—it's the most readily understood, reader-friendly format. Jobs are arranged in a time line, starting with the current or most recent position and working backward, ultimately listing the first job last. People who spend much of their work day reviewing resumes—personnel agency counselors, executive recruiters, and human resources staff—are partial to the chronological format because it makes their job easier. They can easily identify job titles, the names of employers, and dates of employment.

"My clients pay me to find round pegs to go into round holes," says Gilbert Tweed's Tendler Bignell. "So when I see a nontraditional format, I think a candidate is trying to cover up job changes, doesn't have career direction, or [doesn't have] much to sell, so it's easy to eliminate," she says. Chronological resumes are also preferred because the placement of dates next to facts makes reference checking easier.

A chronological format should probably be your choice if you

- Want to make a lateral move to a related functional area within your field;

- Are hoping to change industries (but remain in the same functional area);

- Have worked for employers likely to be known to the people who will be reviewing your resume;

- Are applying for a job in a traditional, conservative field such as banking, accounting, insurance, or law; or

- Have been working in one field or in similar job functions in related fields throughout your career and plan to look for your next position in the same or a related field.

Chronological resumes are not right for everyone, however. "They look good if your career has been linear, but if you have changed direction or experienced a job glitch, they may be seen as evidence of failure," says Right Associates' Chagnon.

The best alternative is a functional resume, that is, one whose main section includes headings by area of expertise followed by a brief work history section and an education section.

Some resume writers, and those who advise them, don't believe it's necessary to use dates to identify when positions were held or skills used. But omitting dates creates problems. The reader can't tell what you did when. "In most cases, I absolutely need to know what a person has been doing most recently and how long ago they used technical skills, [since they] can quickly become outdated," says Jack Schwartz, a New York City–based area managing director for Source Edp, a nationwide data processing recruitment firm.

Even in fields where technical skills are not critical or applicable, employers say they need to be reassured that the job hunter isn't trying to disguise gaps in employment history by using a functional resume. Suggestions for how to make a functional resume time conscious are given in "Create a Working Draft" on page 50.

You might want to consider a functional format if you

- Are a career changer who hopes to put skills learned in one profession to work in a new one (and the relationship between what you have done and what you would like to do isn't obvious), or

- Have worked in a variety of jobs in different fields or functional areas and need to demonstrate connections among your skills and areas of expertise.

The third format option is a combination chronological/functional resume. The primary advantage of a functional resume, its analysis of your strengths by area of expertise, is added to a chronological resume, often as a second page. Why use this format? It's a way to emphasize groups of skills or experience that can help the resume reader more readily see why you are qualified for a position.

Other books on writing resumes include the analytical (or targeted) format, which presents what the job hunter knows and what he or she has done as individual skills and achievements grouped under headings such as "Capabilities" and "Accomplishments." I've decided against presenting this option because most employers don't know what to make of it. And if an employer is having a difficult time getting a handle on you as a candidate, he or she is likely to put your resume aside (and perhaps never get back to reviewing it further) or to put it immediately in the reject pile.

Another problem with an analytical resume is that it doesn't lend itself to easily identifying when the job hunter used the skills or accomplished results he or she has listed. The reason cited most often for using this format—defining experiences so that they fit a specific position—can, I'm convinced, be done more easily and just as effectively with one of the other three formats. You can find examples of each in "Resume Makeovers" on page 101.

Information Sequences Within Formats

Here's the order in which you should list sections of information in a chronological resume.

- Identification (name, address, phone number)
- Job Objective or Summary of Qualifications (both optional)

- Work Experience
- Activities or Professional Involvements/Affiliations (optional)
- Skills (optional)
- Education
- Interests

The exception to this sequence is the resume of a job hunter who is working on or who has recently completed an academic program that is a prerequisite for moving into a new functional area, job level, or industry. If that's your situation, you may want to highlight that experience by putting the Education section before the Work Experience section. It's a judgment call that varies with each situation. If you feel your work experience is more important, feature it first and follow it with your education.

In a functional format, the sequence would be as follows.

- Identification
- Job Objective or Summary of Qualifications (both optional)
- Areas of Expertise
- Work History
- Skills (optional)
- Education
- Interests

For a combination chronological/functional resume, use the chronological format sequence and start your second page with an Identification section followed by an Areas of Expertise section.

If you are unsure of which format is best for you, talk it over with your coach before you begin the next exercise.

Create a Working Draft

Congratulations—you're entering the home stretch. The next step—combining your notes and the marked-up copy of your resume into a legible working draft—will be gratifying because with it you'll see the results of the previous hour of effort.

Using a computer is the best way to compose a draft, but a typewriter is a good second choice. Whoever is the most proficient keyboarder, you or your coach, should input the copy. The other person should watch as the copy is keyed to correct errors and make final editing suggestions. If neither a computer nor a typewriter is available, neatly transfer the copy onto a single sheet of paper to make it easy to read or cut sections from an unmarked copy of your old resume, paste them on the new sheet, and mark revisions by hand.

Don't be concerned at this stage if your resume exceeds one page. You won't know for sure whether all of the copy can comfortably fit in the space you'd like until you've designed it.

What follows is a guide to help you focus on the information each section of your resume should contain. Read the section here that corresponds to the part of your resume you are working on before you actually draft it.

Identification

- Full name (a formal name rather than a nick-name)
- Permanent address (street number and name, apartment number, city, state, and zip code). If you're relocating, it's a good idea to give a local address. If you'll only be at that address temporarily, you may also want to include a second address at which you can receive mail beyond the time you indicate.

EXAMPLE

(Temporary Address 4/92–8/92)   (Permanent Address)
Marriott Residence Inn   6263 Forrest Drive
777 Cypriot Way   Tenafly, NJ 04736
Palo Alto, CA 97801

- Phone number. It must be one where you (or someone who can take a message for you) are available during working hours. If there are times when no one is home, consider investing in an answering machine or hiring a telephone answering service. List your work number if you can comfortably accept a phone call, however brief, from a prospective employer.

If you have included any other personal information—social security number, birth date, marital status, number of dependents, health status, height, or weight—delete it. These details are unnecessary and some may cause you to be ruled out.

Job Objective

Even though you have a written job target, which was used to help develop the content of your resume, it may not be necessary or advisable to include it on the resume itself. Before you decide whether it makes sense in your case, consider some pros and cons.

Pro: A job objective, even a general one, is useful when sending your resume to an employer who is receiving resumes for more than one type of position (almost always the case with personnel departments and departments or divisions of large companies). In short, a job objective is a good way to route a resume to the right person or pile.

Con: A job objective that states the obvious is unnecessary and takes up space. If your career follows a progression well understood in your industry, it makes more sense to talk about the reasons for your interest in a particular job or company in your cover letter.

Pro: A job objective can be useful to the resume reviewer if you're hoping to change job functions, industries, or field or make some other unusual career move. What you choose to emphasize about your experience, of course, should support your candidacy.

Con: A specific objective may narrow your options. If your objective states that you're looking for a position as a paralegal in a litigation department, you may take yourself out of the running if the only current opening at the firm you have applied to is for a paralegal in the corporate department. (That wouldn't be a problem, of course, if you wanted a job involving litigation work only.) One way to avoid the situation is to create more than one resume, each of which features its own unique job objective and emphasizes skills or experiences that support that objective.

If you decide to include a job objective on your resume, keep the following in mind.

- Speak not of what your employer can do for you but what you can do for an employer.
- Be cautious in your use of self-attributed qualities.

- Avoid overused adjectives and phrases that provide no useful information.
- Don't talk about your long-term goals. Mentioning them can be counterproductive, particularly if you say that you'd eventually like to be boss or start your own business.

Summary of Qualifications

The cover letter has traditionally been the place where the job hunter has summarized his or her skills, experiences, and, sometimes, personal qualities. In recent years, however, this information has begun to appear at the top of resumes right after the identification or job objective. Presumably, it's a way to flag the attention of those who may see the resume but not the cover letter. But is it an effective use of space? It all depends on what you say and how you say it. General statements about your work habits and personal qualities are a waste of space.

EXAMPLE

Strong communications skills. Proficient in organization skills and attention to detail. Able to anticipate problems before they arise. Self-motivated, able to work under pressure.

A short, fact-filled summary with statements or examples that back up claims about your abilities, on the other hand, can be effective.

EXAMPLES

Five years of experience as a legal editor/proofreader editing briefs for U.S. federal court cases. A master's degree in English and one year of law school have helped me hone my ability to catch errors of grammar, content, and format. Partners feel comfortable signing off on my work with minimal review. Expert WordPerfect user who, in the words of my boss, "maintains a sense of humor even under the worst deadline pressure."

A senior human resource manager who has worked for three Fortune 500 firms during the last fifteen years, developing expertise in • Employee Relations • Recruiting and Selection • Personnel Administration • Health Plan Administration • Employee Training and Development • Wage and Salary Administration • Outplacement

Work Experience

If you're using the functional format for your resume, read on. If not, and you have decided to use the chronological format, skip ahead to "Describing Past Jobs," on page 58.

You've already identified the main areas of expertise required by your new job target in "What Are You an Expert At" on page 43. Now you need to select the descriptions of tasks or accomplishments from each job you have held and put them under the appropriate heading. Each entry should begin with an action verb. For consistency, it's best to use the past tense of all action verbs, even for current job responsibilities. After each entry, list the year or years you performed or accomplished it. Eliminate job descriptions or accomplishments that don't relate to the kind of position you hope to land.

EXAMPLE

Situation: Kim Pressler has held administrative and teaching jobs at one college since receiving her master's degree from that institution in 1984. Her new job target is a position in event coordination with a corporation or meeting-planning organization. Her current resume, which uses a chronological format, has the following Work Experience section.

Work Experience

Indiana University, Bloomington, Indiana, 1984–present

College Adviser, 1986–present
— Help 150 freshmen plan their curricula
— Initiate tutoring program for students on academic probation
— Coordinate ten major freshman events, including Freshman Family Day, Opening Day Activities, and Freshman Orientation

Program Assistant, Arts and Sciences Division, 1985–86
— Organized faculty committee to review goals and objectives of core curriculum
— Conducted curriculum update workshops for faculty advisers
— Wrote new course catalog for students studying abroad

Instructor, English Department, 1984–85
— Developed and taught remedial writing course, which received faculty recognition at an honors banquet
— Supervised three teaching assistants who graded freshman compositions

Faculty Adviser, Student Activities Office, 1984–85
— Reviewed decisions of elected student officers on bookings of entertainment and cultural events for campus
— Monitored expenditures of $500,000 of student activity fee money

Kim realized that she had experience in four skill areas that related to her next career goal—communications, event coordination, management, and planning. She rearranged the descriptions under her jobs to fit the appropriate categories.

After identifying the areas of expertise of her new job target, Kim grouped her job tasks and accomplishments under the appropriate headings—Events Coordination,

Planning, Communications, and Management. She arranged the categories in order of descending importance and added accomplishments and numbers to support her role in the two top categories, events coordination and planning.

Event Coordination

— Coordinated ten major freshman events involving 1,000 students and a support team of 100 staff and administrators; participation rate jumped to 90–100 percent, exceeding earlier rates of 70–95 percent, 1986–present

— Organized faculty committee to review goals and objectives of core curriculum; the proposals of the committee were unanimously adopted by the president and board of trustees; subsequently asked by several deans to organize such committees for their disciplines, 1985–86

Planning

— Helped 150 freshmen plan their curricula; by working 60-hour weeks over two weeks succeeded in resolving fifty scheduling problems, 1986–present

— Initiated tutoring program for students on academic probation; seventy-five participate each semester, 95 percent of whom go off probation, 1986–present

Communications

— Wrote new course catalog for students studying abroad, 1985–86

— Developed and taught remedial writing course, which received faculty recognition at an honors banquet, 1984–85

— Conducted curriculum update workshops for faculty advisers, 1985–86

Management

— Supervised three teaching assistants who graded freshman compositions, 1984–85
— Reviewed decisions of elected student officers on bookings of entertainment and cultural events on campus, 1984–85
— Monitored expenditures of $500,000 of student activity fee money, 1984–85

If, through your activities, you have developed skills that support your new job target, it's acceptable and advisable to list each under the appropriate area of expertise. It's a good idea to mention the context in which you acquired the skill or got the result.

EXAMPLE

Situation: A job hunter has worked for a few years as a volunteer assisting her pastor in visiting families in which a loved one is dying. She hopes to find a paid position as a hospice counselor with a community organization or hospital.

Counseling

— Served as a volunteer grief counselor to children and their families, 1988 to present

Now, create a job history section. List your job title, the name of the employer, location if necessary (city and state only), and the dates of employment. For additional ideas on how this information can be presented, read the section following the example.

EXAMPLE

Indiana University, Bloomington, Indiana, 1984–present

College Adviser, 1986–present

Program Assistant, Arts and Sciences Division, 1985–86

<u>Instructor</u>, English Department, 1984–85
<u>Faculty Adviser</u>, Student Activities Office, 1984–85

Describing Past Jobs

"Work Experience" is one of the most popular headings used to identify jobs and related tasks. Other options for this section include employment, business history, work history, experience, employment experience, professional experience, and professional background.

Each job subheading should contain job title, company name, and dates of employment. Including a company's location may be important if you have worked in more than one geographic area. It's not necessary to include headings that state the categories (i.e., Job Title, Company, Employer, and Responsibilities); address or phone number of the employer; or the name and title of your manager—these can be included on a separate reference sheet. If your titles reflect the fact that you have steadily advanced in your career, make them the most prominent piece of information in this section.

EXAMPLE

Work Experience
<u>Office Administrator</u>, Jones, Jones & Smith Law Offices, Houston, Texas, 1988–present

If your job titles do not tell as impressive a story as the names of your employers, position that information first.

EXAMPLE

Work Experience
<u>Jones, Jones & Smith Law Offices</u>, Houston, Texas, Office Administrator, 1988–present

Placing dates of employment flush left instead of having them follow the name or location of the employer and indenting the other components is a good choice if you want to emphasize your work continuity.

EXAMPLE

Work Experience

1988–present   Office Administrator, Jones, Jones & Smith Law Offices, Houston, Texas

If you have worked in several positions at one company, it's best to mention the company name and location first, then list the job title and dates you worked in that position.

EXAMPLE

Work Experience

Jones, Jones & Smith Law Offices, Houston, Texas, 1982–present
  Office Administrator, 1988–present
  Bookkeeper, 1985–88
  Receptionist, 1982–85

If the company or companies you worked for are small and/or not likely to be known to the people reviewing your resume, it's smart to add a short description of the company after its name. Another way to handle this is to work the company description into the sentence that describes your responsibilities and accomplishments.

EXAMPLES

Senior Tax Adviser, Crawley Communications, Inc. (a large regional cable television company), Denver, Colorado, November 1988–present

As senior tax adviser for this large regional cable television company, I built a department of five professionals and direct the administration of all income tax planning and compliance.

Four Steps to Tighter Copy

Each time you add a job to your existing resume, it's almost always necessary to ask, "What can I eliminate?" There are four simple ways to consolidate information:

1. Look for repetition. It's most likely to occur in your description of job tasks. Decide where the description is most appropriate and delete the second reference. If, for example, you were a flight attendant and were later promoted to flight service manager, a task that could be repeated under both jobs is: "Ensure strong customer relations through good service."

   Because you're likely to mention more sophisticated tasks in the higher-level job, however, you should word one or more of those so that customer service is implicit. For instance: "Advise or mediate any passenger problems beyond the experience or control of the crew."

2. Bid good-bye to jobs of yore. Pre-career, summer, and part-time jobs you had during school should be the first to bite the dust. It's a good idea to account for where you have worked since you entered the work world full-time, but once a job or group of jobs is no longer relevant to your career, you need only to mention them in a line or two. If you can include accomplishments in these jobs, do.

EXAMPLE

1980–1985   Rose to level of department manager after working in several J. C. Penney stores as a retail salesperson. Was recognized as Department Manager of the Month five times in two years—a store record.

3. Tighten up your draft by eliminating unnecessary words. All of the following are unnecessary.

- Responsible for
- Know how to do
- Involved in
- Worked as a (job title)
- Experienced in
- Conversant in

4. Incorporate accomplishments as clauses in your description of your job tasks.

EXAMPLE

Explained membership benefits to potential health club clients, efforts that resulted in fifty new members in ten months

Education

The further away you get from your college experience, the more selective you should be in what you include about it. By the time you have had three or four jobs, your education section can usually consist of very basic information.

- Degree received. B.A., B.S., M.A., M.S., M.B.A., and Ph.D. are all easily recognized degrees; other degrees should be spelled out unless you are certain the initials will be recognized by people in the field in which you are job hunting.
- University name. If the location is not obvious from the name or its reputation, provide the city and state.
- Year degree was received.
- Major field of study and significant honors (i.e., graduating with distinction or Phi Beta Kappa). It's not necessary to include your grade point average, however spectacular, once your first full-time job is listed on your resume.
- Percentage of education you personally financed through scholarships, part-time work, or

summer jobs. This kind of statement shows that you're a motivated person and that you can successfully juggle more than one commitment at a time—both highly prized qualities in today's workplace. Consider deleting it if you have been out of school five to seven years and need the space to describe more recent accomplishments.

Listing courses you took isn't necessary. However, if they're relevant to the position you're looking for, you can mention them in your cover letter.

If you have received a certificate or degree for completing a program *after* you graduated from college or high school, that information should appear above your college or high school information. You can emphasize the importance of a program or explain the significance of a certificate by adding numbers or a short description.

EXAMPLE

Certificate in Computer Technology, 1985
Merritt College, Oakland, CA (full-time two-year program)

Skills

You've probably noted specific skills when describing your job responsibilities. Highlighting them in a separate section is optional but it's a good idea if they're essential to landing the job you want. It may help to give this section a more specific title—Technical Skills, Hardware and Software Skills, and Office Equipment Skills are among the possibilities.

If you list the names of equipment or software programs, be sure to include the version that you work on (it's usually expressed as a number, as in Microsoft Word 4.0). And be sure to get the spelling and capitalization of the words right; product names often defy the standard rules.

Define your skill level if it makes sense to do so. "Able to write, speak, and translate Spanish," for example, or "Fluent in French; lived in France for five years."

Activities

Including professional activities is always a good idea if you have the space. It shows that you're interested in your field beyond what's called for by your job. If your community or volunteer involvements are significant or provide additional evidence of skills you use as a professional, they're also worth including. How many you choose to include and the detail you provide is a judgment call, but this section shouldn't overwhelm the Work Experience section. The more distant your involvement in a particular activity, the stronger the argument to delete it.

If you decide to include an Activities section, however, it's important to select a heading that announces the kind of information you are presenting. Some of the possibilities are:

- Professional Activities
- Professional Memberships
- Community Activities
- Civic Activities
- Volunteer Work

One of the best ways to give a capsule view of your activities is to list the type of affiliation you have (member, officer, committee chair), the name of the organization (and, if necessary, a brief explanation of what it is), and the dates of your involvement. Another configuration is to start each involvement with an action verb that describes something you did or accomplished.

EXAMPLES

- Coordinated five Boston College alumni events annually, which attracted the best attendance of any local chapter events

- Developed new concept for major PTA fundraiser and, as committee chair, organized fifty volunteers who raised $60,000

If you feel your accomplishments or the skills you developed through your activities will provide further evidence of your qualifications for the job you hope to get, describe them. For instance, a certified public accountant who is hoping to get a position as vice president of taxes at a corporation included the following in her Professional Involvements section.

Tax Executives Institute, member since 1982; Elected president for 1991–1992 term; initiated semiannual meeting focusing on new technology in the field, which drew highest level of participation in organization's history.

If you list college activities on your resume and you've been out of school for three or more years, you should probably eliminate them. If you've been working for three years or less and participated in activities in college that you feel support your career interest and involvement, keep the list short and sweet. Mention the name of the organization, the role you played, and briefly describe your responsibilities or, better yet, a few accomplishments.

EXAMPLE

Situation: A public relations associate at a PR agency who hopes to find a similar job in a Fortune 1000 company.

Media and Publicity Coordinator, Business Roundtable, 1989–90. Efforts resulted in twenty-five mentions in student and local media.

Interests

Some people question whether to include a line or two of information that's not related to their work lives. The employers, recruiters, and outplacement people I consulted say "Do it." Why? Because it's the one place to give the reader of your resume insight into who you are beyond your work identity. More than that, it provides a casual way for the interviewer to start a conversation. And it just may be that the employer shares one of your interests, which can only help you as a candidate. If you have an unusual interest, for example, playing guitar in a Celtic music group or competing in hot air balloon races, it may just capture the fancy of the resume reader and result in his or her wanting to learn more about you.

A simple list of interests, even if it consists of only two items, is fine. It's important to be specific. Saying that you enjoy sports, reading, music, or traveling is not very revealing. It's far better to say: Running 10K races, reading biographies of famous historical figures, listening to 1940s rhythm and blues music, or going on archaeological digs. Another way to define your interests is to put a few words of explanation after each item.

EXAMPLE

Photography (specialize in children's portraits)
Hiking (have completed the Appalachian Trail)
Quilting (have won honorable mentions at three
   exhibitions)

References

It's not necessary to include the line "References Available on Request"—that's a statement of the obvious. You may, however, want to prepare a list of references on a separate piece of paper so that you can give it to a prospective employer once he or she indicates you are in the running for a job. (That could be as early as the end of a first interview, which is a good reason to take the reference sheet with you.) At the top of the sheet, use the same identification heading as you did for your resume. Then center the heading "List of References." Include the following information for each reference you list: the name of your immediate supervisor, his or her job title, phone number, and the name and address of the company.

EXAMPLE

Jeff Levin, Vice President, Customer Service
ABC Direct Marketing
111 North Shore Road
Hempstead, New York 10537
516-555-7200

One statement that you may want to include at the bottom of your resume is "Willing to Relocate" (if you are). Being flexible about where you live may result in being considered for a job in a location other than the one you have applied for.

Why You Shouldn't Tell White Lies

You may be tempted to inflate your job title, fudge dates of employment, or exaggerate your educational credentials in order to come across as a more qualified job candidate. It's *not* a good idea.

Altering the truth can get you into trouble. Employers today often take the time to check out information on resumes. If prospective employers discover inconsistencies, they are likely to bump you off the list immediately. The reasoning? If you lie about your credentials, how can you be trusted as an employee? If the discovery is made after you've been hired, you stand to lose your job. In short, the edge you think you may gain isn't worth the risk.

There *are* ways to present yourself as a strong candidate without telling white lies and jeopardizing your credibility, however. Avoid the temptations listed below by following the accompanying suggestions.

Disguising work gaps. You can't afford to leave an unexplained work gap of more than a few months on your resume, particularly if it's current. If you do, you'll be screened out. You need to explain why you haven't been working. "If there were extenuating circumstances, be up front about what they were," says Edp's Jack Schwartz.

Gaps that are the result of caring for a seriously ill relative, managing a family business or affairs after the death of a parent or sibling, or recovering from an accident or illness yourself are increasingly understood and accepted by employers. The format of a resume does not leave much room for explanation, and more than a clause may be necessary. You should note the gap on your resume and expand on it in a cover letter. Suggestions for what to say about this specific situation are provided in the cover letters section on page 88.

If you have taken time out from your career to raise a family, a line explaining that at the appropriate chronological point is one option: "1986–92—Left full-time employment to raise three children."

If a period of unemployment occurred one or more jobs ago, chances are the gap will not be used to screen you out. "Most hiring managers would assume that the employer or employers who hired you after you were unemployed checked out the gap and did not consider it a problem, so they wouldn't either," says Schwartz.

If you don't want to call attention to a period of unemployment that was in the past, it's acceptable to use only years rather than months and years for employment dates. It's a mistake to omit dates altogether because each reader of your resume can then make up his or her own explanation for the lack. One could presume that you have an addiction or a health problem, or that you leave a job when you're offered more money elsewhere, or that you're older than you really are. The result will be that you won't get a call for an interview.

Changing job titles. The risk of inflating your job title to make your job or responsibilities sound more important than they really are (or were) is that it's easy to get caught. Job titles are one of the few things that personnel departments routinely provide to prospective employers who inquire. If, however, your title doesn't accurately reflect the scope and importance of your responsibilities, you can change it to make it more accurately reflect what you do. To avoid the possibility of any misunderstanding, you should clarify what you did at your interview, that is, mention that your actual job was X, but that you took the liberty of making it clearer in the wording on your resume.

Inventing academic credentials. It's downright dangerous to claim you attended or graduated from a particular school if you didn't—just as bad is awarding yourself a degree you never earned. If a help-wanted ad or posted job requires a certain educational background, be honest about your credentials and explain in your cover letter why you should nonetheless be considered.

Exaggerating your capabilities. Being self-confident is a plus, but overstating your knowledge or expertise on paper not only may cause embarrassment if you're asked a technical question during the interview but may result in your being written off as a fraud.

Taking more credit than is yours. It's fine to describe your contributions to a successful project, but saying that you initiated, supervised, or were solely responsible for something when that was not really the case is foolish. It's too easy for a prospective employer to discover what your real role was through a conversation with your former boss, colleagues, or people you both know. At the very least, your credibility will suffer, and in the worst-case scenario, you'll be dismissed as a candidate.

Claiming free-lance or consultant status. You should claim such status only if you really were engaged in such efforts;

otherwise, you won't have legitimate answers about questions an employer is likely to ask about your "business."

Resume Length: How Long Is Too Long?

Ask ten regular readers of resumes how long a resume should be and you'll get a split vote. Half will say one page is enough for anyone and half will say they can handle resumes that are up to three pages long. But remember, the only professionals who can get away with longer resumes are professors, psychologists, doctors, and others who are expected to list published articles, research, or conference presentations.

I prefer a one-page resume because it shows the job seeker knows how to highlight and organize material, and there's no chance that any pages will be lost when the staple or paper clip proves ineffective. Today's word processing and desktop publishing software programs allow you to get a lot of copy on one page and still have a great looking resume.

Time for this exercise: Total time:
5 minutes   90 minutes

Perfect Your Copy

The final step before you design your resume is to make sure that the copy is in its best final form. You and your coach should go through the following checklist together and look for and mark omissions, repetitions, misspellings, and typographical errors on your draft. If you're unsure about the rationale or options for any of the items mentioned on the checklist, go back to "Create a Working Draft" on page 50.

If you're working on a computer, use the word processing program's spell-checking feature to spot typographical and spelling errors, and double check with a sight check. After all, if "to" is keyed instead of "two," it will not be caught by the spell checker because while the usage is incorrect, the spelling is correct.

Copy Checklist

IDENTIFICATION INFORMATION

What's needed:
☐ Full name
☐ Address (temporary and permanent with dates)
☐ Daytime phone number

What isn't needed:
Social security number
Marital status

Number of dependents
Height, weight, and other physical characteristics
Work availability
Health status
Date of birth

JOB OBJECTIVE
(Optional)

What's needed:

☐ Short statement (no more than two lines) in clear, specific language

SUMMARY OF QUALIFICATIONS
(Optional)

What's needed:

☐ Precise listing of skills or areas of expertise
☐ Personal qualities backed up by examples or attributed by others
☐ Three-line maximum

SECTION HEADINGS

What's needed:

☐ Correct sequence
☐ Consistency in placement

WORK EXPERIENCE

What's needed:

☐ Clauses, not complete sentences
☐ Current job responsibilities in present tense (except in functional format—use past tense)
☐ Past job responsibilities in past tense
☐ Acronyms or abbreviations spelled out
☐ Different action verbs so none appears more than once

What's not needed:
Employer phone number
Name of supervisor
The phrases "responsible for" or "duties included"
The headings "Position," "Job Title," or "Duties"
Capitalizing words unnecessarily
Redundant job tasks
References to salary
Reasons for leaving past job

Accomplishments

What's needed:
☐ Job, time frame, or context in which each occurred
☐ Numbers to quantify
☐ Solid analysis of results
☐ Specifics
☐ Examples

What's not needed:
Self-congratulatory wording

In a functional format

What's needed:
☐ Three or four areas of expertise as main section headings
☐ Three or four entries listed under each heading

EDUCATION

What's needed:
☐ Name of certificate/degree received and year/month awarded
☐ Major field of study (optional)

What's not needed:
Course work (unless recent and relevant to position you are applying for)

**If graduation from college was within
the last five years list**

☐ Major scholarships/awards received
☐ Percentage of college expenses earned through
  summer or part-time jobs
☐ Honors received (optional)

ACTIVITIES
(Optional)

What's needed:

☐ Name of organization (several-word explanation if
  necessary)
☐ Brief description of role you played
☐ Dates of involvement
☐ Accomplishments (with numbers to quantify)

What's not needed:

Activities not recent or relevant to job target

SKILLS
(Optional)

What's needed:

☐ One- or two-word description of skill and skill level
☐ Correctly spelled names of software programs,
  hardware, and other equipment

INTERESTS

What's needed:

☐ Brief descriptions of specific activities

As you no doubt noticed, your 90 minutes are up and
your content should be in perfect condition. Space may
ultimately dictate decisions on whether to include or leave
out certain entries. You'll still have an opportunity to cut
material once you have designed your resume—the next
step.

Design Your Resume

What your resume says is important, but unless it looks inviting, it may not get more than a glance from potential employers. Until a few years ago, it was fine to type your resume and have it reproduced on bond paper—the number of job hunters who had their resumes typeset was low. Now, however, more and more job hunters are using word processing or desktop publishing programs to produce resumes with presentations that make their typed counterparts look like plain cousins.

A graphically pleasing resume is worth the extra time or money to produce, especially when competition for jobs is keen. Making your resume a visual success is something you can easily do, particularly if you know a word processing program such as Microsoft Word or WordPerfect and have a computer you can access. If you don't, there are two options: pay someone to input it for you, or rent a computer at a copy shop that has resume design templates available and input it yourself. Many copy shops, including AlphaGraphics Print Shops and Kinko's Copies, both of which have franchises nationwide, will design resumes from handwritten or typed copy. They can also design resumes from copy that has already been input on a disk, which reduces the chance of the designer making typographical errors and may cost less since inputting copy is time consuming. Fees for this service vary across the country but on the average range from $30 to $90 for a one-page resume and $40 to $110 for a two-page resume. Some copy shops will also sell you a duplicate disk with your resume on it for a minor charge, which enables you to update it on disk whenever necessary. Be sure to ask what word processing or desktop publishing program—and which version—was used to create the resume document and label the disk.

The second option, using a resume template and inputting the copy yourself, is available at AlphaGraphics. Doing this requires no computer know-how, just keyboarding skills. You pay by the hour to use a Macintosh—the rate ranges from $8 to $20. If you're not a good typist, keep in mind that keying it yourself could end up costing you more than having a design specialist do the whole job.

If you've decided to have someone else design your resume, skip ahead to "Getting Your Resume into the Hands of Decision Makers" on page 85.

A Primer on Design

You don't need to be a graphic designer to design a terrific-looking resume. If you know little or nothing about design, however, you may inadvertently make a beginner's mistakes, such as using more than one typeface. But knowing a lot about design can get you in trouble, too, because you may be tempted to show off your expertise and overdo it.

"Keep one word in mind as you lay out your resume— KISS—or 'keep it simple, stupid,'" says Barbara Stafford, a graphic designer and manager of the electronic graphics department at AlphaGraphics' commercial printing division. "The challenge is to make the text inviting and readable, not to dazzle the resume reader with fancy graphic sleights of hand."

Her advice makes a lot of sense; after all, a resume is as highly developed a form as a business letter. Here's how to create a great-looking resume in six steps:

Select the right typeface and point size. You may be limited in your choice of typeface or font by what is available on the software program you are using. Microsoft Word 4.00B, for example, offers a choice of eight typefaces. Typefaces that are not included in your software can be purchased separately and added to it. You may choose a serif font, which features short cross lines at the ends of the main strokes of the letters, or a sans scrif font, which does not.

EXAMPLE

Serif font: Md   *Sans serif font:* Md

The following is a list of typefaces that are highly recommended for resumes. The names may differ slightly (i.e., Times, Times Roman, or Times New Roman), depending on the company that produced the type for the software program, and they may look slightly different but not enough to be noticed by an untrained eye.

Serif Fonts

Times—a condensed typeface that's a good choice if you need to get a lot of text on a page.

New Century Schoolbook—a wide typeface that's a good choice if you want to expand your text and fill out a page.

Palatino—a typeface that's more distinctive than its close relative, Times.

Bookman—another wide typeface that's a good choice if you want to expand your text and fill out a page.

Sans Serif Fonts

Helvetica and Helvetica Narrow—a legible, geometric typeface; Helvetica Narrow allows you to get more text on the page.

Optima—a thick and thin typeface that's distinctive and not as widely used as other typefaces mentioned here.

Univers—the equivalent of Helvetica and Helvetica Narrow for IBM PCs and compatibles.

Avoid using a script font, because it is too hard to read.

EXAMPLE

It's best to avoid a script font

The point size—the specification for the size of the type—should be a 10- or 12-point size for the body of your resume. You might start with 10 point if you think you'll have trouble getting everything on one page. You shouldn't go smaller than a 9-point size, or some resume readers will have to strain to make out the letters.

Headings should be a consistent size and be in proportion to the text size. Use a 14-point size for all headings if you use 12 point for the text, use a 12-point size if you use 10 point for the text. Avoid the temptation to enlarge your name to a huge point size that will look disproportionate. An 18-point size is the largest you should use if you use 14-point headings, a 14-point size is fine if you use 12-point headings. Subheadings (job title, employer, degree earned, college attended) should be set in the same point size as the text that follows it.

Be consistent about the placement of section headings. You can pull the resume reader's eye to your name by centering it on the page. Your name and address can go directly underneath. If you are listing more than one address, you may want to put one on the left side and one on the right and indicate the dates when you can be reached at each.

Because we read from left to right, it makes aesthetic and practical sense to position all your headings flush left. Centered headings are less desirable. All entries under all subheadings should be indented the same amount of space. Second or wraparound lines may be indented more.

Keep graphic elements minimal. To highlight your headings, use boldface, capital letters, italic (only if it is easy to read), or underline. If you're creating a functional resume, incorporate a slightly different graphic element for the major areas of expertise than you use for other headings.

EXAMPLE

Section headings:	Areas of Expertise:
WORK HISTORY	**Administration**
EDUCATION	**Management**
INTERESTS	**Marketing**

For subheadings (job title, employer, dates of employment), use only one or two of the four elements suggested here. Using three elements at a time—for instance, underlining, italic, and boldface—is overkill. Avoid outlining or shadowing letters; they make copy hard to read.

EXAMPLE

Work Experience

<u>Media Planner</u>, Young & Rubicam, New York, New York, 6/85–9/89

Each entry under a subheading should be indented and set off with a simple graphic element so that the eye moves quickly and easily down the page. Blocks of copy that use only periods as punctuation are more difficult to read. Bullets are a good way to introduce items under headings, provided they do not dwarf the size of the type.

If you're working on a Macintosh, you can create a bullet with any software program by depressing the "Option" and "8" keys. On an IBM or IBM-compatible with Microsoft Windows software, depress the "ALT" key and type "0215" on the numeric keypad.

EXAMPLE

Functional resume:

Presentation

- Provided commentary for audiovisual and multimedia slide shows, ranging in length from 5 to 30 minutes
- Moderated panel discussions of experts, including members of Congress, religious leaders, and college presidents

Dashes, triangles, or squares are fine for setting off copy too, but avoid the temptation to use the many icons and symbols that software makes available, such as snowflakes, stars, or pointing fingers. They detract from the simplicity and form of a resume.

The only place a line across the whole page belongs, should you choose to use one, is after the Identification section and before the first major heading.

EXAMPLE

Rose Harrigan
52 Main Street
Bath, Ohio 44020
(216) 555-3190

WORK EXPERIENCE

Using a border to frame your copy is a mistake, say graphic designers. It pulls the eye of the reader away from the text, which should be the main attraction.

Build in white space. The easiest way to make sure your resume doesn't look too cluttered is to allow a 1-inch margin on all four sides and to create what's known in design as leading (extra space) between your headings. The greatest leading should be between the Identification section and the first heading.

If you have plenty of white space to manipulate, it's preferable to have more space at the bottom than at the top. Don't increase the leading between headings, or your resume will look too spread out. For most people, the problem will be too little space. If that's what you've found, reducing the margins to a half inch all around may increase what you can get on a page. If you try this and you still have too much copy, you can reduce the point size (from 12 to 10 or 10 to 9) and bring the margins back to 1 inch. If that doesn't work, reduce the margins again. Remember, don't go smaller than a 9-point type size or set less than one-half-inch margins. It's better to cut copy or create a second page.

Make a sophisticated paper choice. There are three elements to consider: weight, finish, and color. The most commonly used resume papers are 20-pound bond or 50-pound offset (both weights are the same) in a linen (textured) or laid (flat) finish.

If you want the Mercedes Benz of the paper world, go for a 24-pound Nekoosa, Classic Linen, or Becket Cambric. A 24-pound paper is thicker and has more texture than 20-pound bond or 50-pound offset. Don't go overboard in your search for a paper that will stand out in the crowd. A heavy cover stock or gloss finish, for example, will stand out, but for the wrong reasons. Ditto for color choices other than neutral ones. Different shades of white, grey, and beige are classy and show sophistication.

The best way to decide on a paper is to ask your local copy shop to show you the ones mentioned above and other similar papers. You should buy extra sheets of the same paper to use for cover letters. Envelopes should also match.

Reproduce your resume so that each one looks like an original. The best choices are the high-quality professional copiers used in copy shops (for large quantities) or laser printers (especially if you intend to customize individual resumes, send out a limited quantity, or have produced several resumes, each with a different job target).

Final Design Dos and Don'ts

- DO strive for consistency in your use of graphic elements. For example, if you capitalized your first job title, subsequent job titles should also be capitalized.

- DO insist on proofreading the final copy several times (and have someone else whose judgment you trust do the same) *before* it's printed.
- DO use black ink.
- DON'T mix typefaces.
- DON'T produce a two- or four-color resume to show off your design repertoire.
- DON'T use screened images behind the type.
- DON'T include a photograph unless you are an actor or actress.

A Word on Unique Resumes

Unique resumes can get an employer's attention. And sometimes they favorably impress an employer. But the arguments against trying to create a unique resume are powerful. (1) Unless you have graphic design training, your efforts are likely to look amateurish. (2) Your unique design (an oversize resume, for example) may prove problematic because it doesn't easily fit in a resume stack. Set aside, it may be forgotten or trashed. (3) Your attempt to be clever, avant-garde, or humorous may be misinterpreted.

If you do, however, decide to put a design spin on your resume, it will work best if there's a reason for doing so. One resume writer with twenty-five years of experience created a design that complemented her text and allowed her to get more information on her resume than a standard 8½-by-11-inch sheet would permit. She used an 11-by-13 piece of paper and folded it widthwise so that the paper conformed to the normal 8½-by-11-inch sheet of paper. In doing so, she created a partial cover, which contained her identification information; the other side of it featured her skills by functional area. The main part was reserved for a traditional chronological resume. To fit all the information she wanted to include, the other alternative would have been to use a second sheet of paper, so this design alternative served her purpose well—and there was no chance of one page getting detached from the other.

Nevertheless, your time will probably be better spent doing basic job search legwork: identifying potential employers, meeting with people in those organizations who are in a position to advise or help you, and contacting decision makers by sending your resume, a carefully thought-out cover letter, and following up with a phone call.

Putting Your
Resume to Work

Getting Your Resume into the Hands of Decision Makers

Once the final version of your resume is reproduced, you'll be armed with your most important job-hunting tool: You. Now that you have analyzed your skills and accomplishments on paper, you should feel more confident about discussing them with potential employers.

Based on hundreds of interviews with employers, recruiters, employment counselors, and job hunters over the last twenty years, I believe that a well-written resume can be extremely helpful in a job search whether it is used to get an interview, to familiarize those involved in the hiring process with who you are, or to follow up an interview.

Too often, however, job hunters use their resume as a crutch. They figure if they send out enough copies to employers, someone somewhere is going to say, "This is the perfect person for us." No way, José. Getting an interview isn't that easy, at least not usually. You'll have far more success if you're highly selective about where and to whom you send your resume—identifying companies, divisions, departments, and people who have a need for someone with your skills and background.

Responding to help-wanted ads is fine, but you can't afford to make that the focus of your efforts. It's essential for you to contact people who are in a position to provide information about job leads and the hiring process at their company and who can put you in touch with those who have the power to hire you. Give them a copy of your resume so they can speak knowledgeably about your skills and accomplishments. Who are these people? They can be

- Friends, friends of your parents, neighbors, and relatives. They know you and are the most likely prospects to offer to go out of their way to help you.
- Ex-colleagues. Track them down if they've changed employers—they can be one of your biggest sources of job leads.
- People you know through social, school, athletic, or community organizations. If they aren't in a position to put you in touch with a job contact, they may know someone who can.
- Colleagues in professional organizations. It pays to be discreet if you're job hunting, so you should pass your resume on only to those you can trust to keep it quiet.
- Alumni resume databanks. At many colleges and universities, the placement or alumni office tries to link up job hunting alumni with employers.

Be sure to follow up on every suggestion. Get the spelling of every person's name, his or her job title, company, and phone number. Write down how your contact knows the person suggested and ask if it's all right for you to use his or her name. If you're not sure how the suggested person might be helpful to you in your job search, ask your contact for more information. It's almost always best to call rather than write. (If you can get the person on the line, you'll get immediate feedback.) After you talk, follow up with a thank-you letter and a copy of your resume. If you've arranged to see the person, take copies of your resume with you.

Beyond Networking

Using the telephone and library to target employers is a task many job hunters prefer to skip because it's time consuming and can be tedious or because they don't know their way around a library. But every hour you invest in locating and learning about potential employers will increase your chances for an interview and your chances to be hired. Your goal should be to develop a list of dozens of employers who hire people with your skills and experience. You can start your research at home with the *Yellow Pages*. Headings in it are straightforward—"Banks," "Lawyers," "Restaurants." If you're looking for a job in a field that doesn't directly service consumers (i.e., machine tooling), check the business-to-business section. In large cities, this may be a separate directory. Copy down the name, address, and telephone number of prospective employers.

Your next step is a trip to the business section of the local library. Don't be intimidated if you haven't used it before. You'll find most librarians eager to assist you. To add to your list of prospective employers, ask for the following reference books.

- *Standard & Poor's Register of Corporations, Directors, and Executives,* published by McGraw-Hill, volume 2 lists companies by location.
- *The National Directory of Addresses and Phone Numbers,* published by Gale Research Inc.
- *Million Dollar Directory,* published by Dun & Bradstreet, volume 3 lists businesses geographically.
- *Job Seeker's Guide to Private and Public Companies,* published by Gale Research Inc.

If you know the industry you want to work in, you should also ask the librarian to recommend a specific reference book. If you want to work for a law firm, for example, *The Martindale-Hubbell Law Directory* would be a good starting point.

Next, identify the manager in each company or organization on your list who heads up the division or department you hope to work in. Some reference books provide this information, but because people often change positions, your best bet is a phone call to the company switchboard. Ask the operator for the exact spelling of the person's name and his or her job title. To keep your phone costs down, get an 800 directory (i.e., the business edition of the *AT&T Toll-Free Directory*).

Now you can begin writing cover letters.

The Secrets of a Successful Cover Letter

Sending a resume without an accompanying letter is like giving a gift with no card—it's incomplete and can be confusing. You stand a much better chance of being invited for an interview if you take the trouble to briefly explain why you are writing to a particular employer. If you find the prospect of writing a cover letter intimidating, the following suggestions can make the process simpler.

Write to a specific person. It's far better to target someone at the department you'd like to work in who has the power to hire than it is to send your letter to someone in personnel. A manager receives far fewer resumes and is more likely to at least skim yours even if he or she isn't currently hiring. Even if it ends up getting passed on to personnel, it may get more attention (particularly if the manager attaches a positive comment) than one that was sent directly to personnel.

Explain your interest. In the first paragraph, mention how you heard about the job opening or why you are interested in applying for a job with the company. Try to be as specific as you can—say that you saw the company's ad, that a mutual friend recommended you contact the person, that an employee told you about plans for expansion. Be sure to get permission to name the people you refer to. If possible, discuss why the work of the department or company is of particular interest to you.

Avoid using phrases that sound canned or disingenuous, such as "your xyz department is the best one in the industry" or "working for a company such as yours, with its excellent reputation." Instead, attempt to relate your interests to the products or services of the employer: "Having been an amateur astronomer since high school, I would welcome the opportunity to use my promotional skills in the public relations department of the planetarium."

Describe your credentials. Don't lift parts of your resume and insert them into the cover letter. Instead, decide which skills, accomplishments, or experiences are particularly relevant to what the employer is looking for and describe them, incorporating terminology the employer has used in a help-wanted ad, written job description, or conversation, if possible. It's a good idea to refer back to your fact sheets or to the working draft of your resume to get ideas on language or details worth incorporating.

If, for example, the employer is looking for a sales professional with at least one year's experience in office equipment markets, a job hunter could explain his or her experience as follows. "After completing a six-month training program, I competed with experienced sales people in the computer hardware business and was named second runner-up in the Top Sales Person of the Year award among a sales force of fifty." Mentioning three key credentials is plenty. After all, the purpose of the cover letter is to pique the interest of the employer.

State what you can do for the company. The purpose of the third paragraph is to set you apart as an applicant who understands the employer's needs, not as someone who is simply looking to better his or her own situation. You might write, "I'm confident that I can use my writing and presentation skills to increase attendance at the planetarium and would be prepared to share my ideas on how that might be done in an interview" or "I would enjoy the opportunity to put my selling skills to work for a company whose product line I'm already familiar with because of my experience."

The more you understand about the current business situation of the employer you'll be talking to, the easier it will be to know how to talk about what you can do for that company. Articles that have been written within the last year about the industry or the employer are often the best sources of information and are easy to locate.

If you subscribe to a database information service such as CompuServe, Dialog, or Prodigy, you can search for article citations and summaries on your computer. A less expensive alternative is to visit your local library. You may be able to use its computer or CD-ROM disks to do similar searches or you can use standard reference books such as the *Business Periodicals Index*, the *New York Times Index*, or the *Wall Street Journal Index*.

If the prospective employer is a publicly traded company, call and request a copy of its annual report from its public relations or corporate communications department. Annual reports often describe organization structures and provide photos of office and plant facilities.

Ask for an interview. If you haven't already mentioned that you would like a chance to meet in person, as was the case in the planetarium example, add a sentence that requests an interview. Saying that you have ideas about how to improve the employer's service or product—particularly if you know it has been targeted by the employer as an area of concern—is a good way to couch a request instead of simply stating, "I hope we have an opportunity to meet." You might also indicate when it's easiest to reach you, whether it's all right for the employer to contact you at work, and when you'll be following up with a check-in phone call.

Sample Cover Letter

3231 33rd Street, N.W.
Washington, DC 20028

June 1, 1991

Mr. Dukes Dunphy
Director, Sports Equipment Marketing
XYZ Corporation
111 Third Avenue
New York, New York 10022

Dear Mr. Dunphy:

The recent story about your company's new product offerings in *Crain's New York Business* caught my attention. In it, you were quoted as saying that you anticipated adding a staff member or two when you introduce your new line of golf products. I feel that I could help make that launch a success.

Here's why: I have been an avid golfer for twenty years and have won many regional tournaments. Beyond that, I have ten years of experience as a marketing specialist with a computer electronics retailer. How can a guy with marketing expertise in a different product line do a good job for you? Let me answer with a brief description of a recent accomplishment.

One year ago, the CEO of my company invited all senior managers to submit ideas on how to increase our store's visibility and image, particularly among 35- to 45-year-old men. My idea, a products/store promotional tie-in with ten sporting events (including two golf tournaments) in the metropolitan area, was implemented with great success. We were able to measure increased store visits (50 percent in the two-week period measured) and increased sales (35 percent) with a coupon that was part of our sports program giveaway.

I feel that I can get similar results with your new product line. I will call you within the week to find out if we can arrange a time to talk.

Sincerely,

Dale Robinson
(202-555-0155)

Use a professional-looking design. Be sure that the design and look of your cover letter are as professional and inviting as your resume. You can achieve this if you do the following.

- Use the same type and size of paper as you did for your resume. Personal stationery, paper with the letterhead of your current (or past) employer, or plain typing paper are taboo.
- Use the same typeface as you did on your resume. For a long cover letter, a 10-point typeface will look best. For a short letter, a 12-point typeface is fine.
- Set up the letter using traditional business-letter techniques. The preferred format is to align your address, the date, the closing, and your name and phone number at the center of the page. The employer's name, address, and the salutation should be flush left.

Don't forget to proofread your letter and, if you are composing it on a computer, use its spell checking feature, too.

How to Address Work Gaps

If you are unemployed and have been searching for a job without success for months rather than weeks, you should address the situation in your cover letter. It would help to explain, for example, that you and twenty-five of your colleagues with virtually identical skills and experiences were let go when your employer reorganized. Or if you were given severance and have the luxury of waiting for just the right job offer or have turned down offers that were not quite right, write that. It's also a good idea to emphasize the positive things you did during a work gap, whether it was helping out in a family business, playing an active role in your child's school, taking courses or seminars to improve skills, or learning a new software program.

The bottom line, of course, is to reassure the employer that you are a valuable, hard-working, upbeat candidate he or she cannot afford to ignore.

How to Respond to a Request for Salary Information

Don't reveal your current salary or salary history (it's to your advantage in a salary negotiation to have the employer tell you the range first). If the employer or help-wanted ad to which you are replying specifically requests such information, you're better off saying that you're looking for a salary that's in line with the going rate for someone with your experience. (In a recent survey conducted by Fox-Morris Associates, a Philadelphia-based executive search and outplacement consulting firm, almost 80 percent of human resource executives reported that they would call an applicant whose resume interested them, even if the person was outside an advertisement's salary guidelines.) You may be concerned that a potential employer will rule you out because you work in an area where salaries are high. One option is to say that you're willing to accept a salary commensurate with your experience and in line with salaries in the area in which the employer is located.

A Final Word

I hope that you feel confident and optimistic about starting your job search as a result of reading *The Advanced 90-Minute Resume* and working through the process. Keep in mind that finding the right job may take weeks or months of looking. If you are not successful in getting interviews, you may have to become more aggressive in tracking down leads by talking to as many connected people as you can about what you are looking for. Or you may have to expand your geographic or career boundaries.

Don't get discouraged if you get rejection after rejection. You need only one "yes" to get a new job. And the more "no's" you hear, the better the odds are that it won't be long before you get that "yes."

Career Decision Resources

Career Counseling: Rx for Career Confusion

Are you unable to find a new job at your level in the industry you've been in for years? Have you lost interest in your career? Are you unhappy in your current job but aren't sure why? Do you feel you need objective coaching on what your next career move ought to be? A career counselor may be the doctor you need to cure your malaise.

A number of resources are available to help you find career counseling services. They include:

- Friends and colleagues. Ask whether they know of any counselors. A satisfied client is often the best indication of an effective counselor.

- The career information office of the adult education division of a local college. Contact staff and workshop leaders. They often do one-on-one counseling.

- The job information services division of the local library. Call to see if it offers free one-on-one counseling. If it doesn't, the staff may be able to refer you to counseling sources.

- *What Color Is Your Parachute?* by Richard Nelson Bolles. Check the state-by-state listings of individuals and agencies mentioned in Appendix C.

- *Yellow Pages.* Check the listings under the headings, "Vocational Guidance" or "Career Services."

Once you have identified one or more possible counselors, call to arrange a phone or in-person interview. Be sure to find out the following:

What are the counselor's credentials? A graduate degree in counseling or in a social science field such as social work, human services, or psychology is a plus, although it doesn't guarantee that the person is an effective counselor. Counseling done as part of his or her training is an indication of competence. An indication of professionalism is whether the counselor is certified by the National Career Development Association. Such certification requires a graduate degree in counseling or a related field, completion of a supervised counseling experience, at least three years of full-time work in the field, and passing a written examination.

Who are the counselor's clients? Find out how closely their backgrounds and problems parallel yours. If, for example, the counselor has worked extensively with students and you are someone with a lot of work experience, it may not be the best match.

What can the counselor do for you? Briefly describe your career problem and have the counselor suggest which services he or she feels are most appropriate. These might include individual or group counseling, testing, and exercises to improve decision-making or job-hunting skills. If you have a "where do I go from here?" problem, an experienced counselor will want to gather all types of information about you—your interests, aptitudes, skills, values, and goals—before beginning the career planning process.

How much will it cost? It's smart to compare the fees of several counselors to get an idea of what the going rate is. Be wary of any counselor who insists on charging you for a package of services. Make sure that you can stop at any time with the understanding that you'll only pay for the services already provided.

Be wary of counselors who make promises of more money, a better job, or immediate solutions to your career dilemma. The best a good counselor can do is provide you with the tools to make your own decisions and help you figure out strategies that will work for you.

Computers: An On-Line Solution for a Career Crisis

If you are at a crossroads in your career because you have had no luck finding a job in your field, are burned out because of the stress or emotional demands of your current job, or are just plain bored doing what you're doing, you owe it to yourself to figure out what your options are.

One of the ways to get a handle on how to channel your interests, skills, and experiences into a new career or industry is to use a career software program. Two of the most widely available ones are SIGI PLUS (System for Interactive Guidance and Information Plus More) from the Educational Testing Service and DISCOVER from the American College Testing Program. Both are user friendly. You need not have any computer or keyboarding skills to use them. Both feature self-assessment exercises; create personalized lists of occupations based on the user's values, interests, skills, and level of education; and provide information about careers and the preparation each requires.

SIGI PLUS can also help users estimate their chances of completing the education or training required for a particular career, decide what their chances of getting into a particular occupation will be, and put their plan into action. DISCOVER offers information on graduate schools. Both programs are widely available in college career-planning and placement offices. If you are an alumnus of a college, you may be able to use your school's software. They may also be available through your local library.

Another program, CAREER DESIGN, produced by Atlanta-based Career Design Software, offers job research strategies and methods for improving presentation skills, including proposal, letter, and resume writing. The user who is unsure of what the next best step in his or her career should be is advised to go through the program's complete sequence, a process that can take three to four days at the computer, plus at least as many days visiting people who can help in a job search. If the user is not willing to commit himself or herself to that much time, there are seven other recommended sequences of various lengths, including one for those who know what they want to do but need help identifying potential employers.

CAREER DESIGN can be purchased for about $100 and installed on an IBM PC or compatible. The user manual provides clearly written instructions for using the features of the program. If you can't find CAREER DESIGN in a software store, write or call Career Design Software, P.O. Box 95624, Atlanta, GA 30347, 800-346-8007.

Resume Makeovers

90-Minute Results

The sample resumes that appear in this section have been adapted from real resumes. Each is depicted before and after the job hunter went through the 90-minute process, and analyscs of the biggest faults of the "before" version and of the strong points of the "after" version are provided.

Chronological Format

Moving Up

Paula has worked for eight years in management capacities in different types of restaurants. Her job target is to find a job as manager of a large restaurant in a major hotel chain in a resort setting. Since the logical progression of her experience leads to that target, she decided not to include it on the resume itself.

ANALYSIS

Paula's "before" resume is difficult to read because she has a single block of copy under each job. She provides some numbers to help quantify the scope of her responsibilities but could easily include more. She hints at the results of her efforts but does not spell them out clearly.

It's much easier to read Paula's revised resume, which, with the use of graphic elements, better spacing, and a computer typeface, is more professional looking. She has dropped some of her less important job tasks and included details about her accomplishments, making her a much stronger candidate on paper. (Typeface: Helvetica)

Before

Paula Sawbridge
6666 Coleridge Ave.
Palo Alto, California 94873
(415) 555-6784

PROFESSIONAL HISTORY:
Food & Beverage Manager, Marriott Corporation, Palo
    Alto, California, 1989-present
Institutional food service manager for corporate
conference center responsible for budgets, personnel,
purchasing, and cost control. Revamped menus, product
merchandising, and promotions opening the facility to
new sources of revenue. Directed all areas of
operation of 350-seat dining room, lounge, and
catering. Coordinated summer youth training program,
employee cross-training, and program for handicapped
adults. Wrote departmental standard operating
procedures and policy manual.

Manager, Ship Ahoy Restaurant, Milwaukee, Wisconsin,
    1987-1989
Supervised dining rooms and staff; coordinated
advertising; managed group sales, special events, and
promotions for this floating-barge restaurant.
Initiated campaign to increase check averages through
employee training and beverage promotions.

Manager, Giovanni's Restaurant, Hilton Head Island,
    South Carolina, 1985-1987
Supervised operation of 150-seat restaurant and
directed opening of New York-style catering business
in second outlet. Coordinated advertising, generated
press releases and special event promotions. Developed
new marketing plan and budget.

Assistant Manager, Winberie's Restaurant (Stouffer
    Restaurant Company), Denver, Colorado, 1983-1985
Assisted in management of operation of 150-seat
restaurant. Helped train twenty new employees.
Developed weekly schedule for thirty employees and
resolved scheduling problems. Helped oversee major
kitchen reconstruction.

EDUCATION
1983—B.A., University of Massachusetts at Amherst,
    Hotel and Restaurant Management.

After

Paula Sawbridge
6666 Coleridge Ave.
Palo Alto, California 94873
(415) 555-6784

PROFESSIONAL EXPERIENCE
Food and Beverage Manager
Marriott Corporate Conference Center, Palo Alto, California, 1989–present
- Direct all areas of operation of 350-seat dining room, lounge, and catering service, including budgets, personnel, purchasing, and cost control
- Introduced staff training programs to improve service and spa cuisine menu, both of which played major roles in increasing business 20 percent during my tenure
- Convinced management to back a $25,000 promotion aimed at foreign companies doing business in the Bay Area, resulting in fifteen new clients who booked a total of sixty days at the center in 1991
- Coordinated summer youth training program and program for handicapped adults, which resulted in five new hires; all have since been recognized as employees of the month

Manager
Ship Ahoy Restaurant, Milwaukee, Wisconsin, 1987–1989
- Supervised twenty-five staff members who served three dining rooms seating 250
- Coordinated advertising, managed group sales, special events, and promotions for this floating-barge restaurant; efforts resulted in 15 percent increase in business annually
- Initiated campaign to increase check averages through employee training and beverage promotions; daily averages rose $30 per employee

Manager
Giovanni's Restaurant, Hilton Head Island, South Carolina, 1985–1987
- Supervised operation of 150-seat restaurant
- Directed opening of New York–style catering business, which added 10 percent annually to restaurant profits
- Developed new marketing plan, which helped increase lunch business 25 percent

Assistant Manager
Winberie's Restaurant (Stouffer Restaurant Company), Denver, Colorado, 1983–1985
- Assisted in management of operation of 150-seat restaurant
- Helped train twenty new employees in service, bartending, and busing skills
- Developed weekly schedule for thirty employees
- Helped oversee $100,000 kitchen reconstruction

EDUCATION
1983—B.A., Hotel and Restaurant Management, University of Massachusetts at Amherst

INTERESTS
Photographing wildlife; photos featured in ten major exhibits

Chronological Format

Changing Industries

Jack has developed marketing expertise by working for three different types of manufacturers. He hopes to change industries again. His resume needs to reflect his versatility and his ability to quickly absorb product information and understand a market.

ANALYSIS

Jack's "before" resume gives only sketchy information about his job tasks—there are no numbers to give the reader an idea of the scope of his responsibilities, and he hasn't told what happened as a result of his efforts. In the blurbs about his employers, he doesn't offer any clues about the kind of manufacturers they were or products he represented. The design of his resume limits what he can write as does using the first person and constructing complete sentences.

By introducing more details in his revised resume, including descriptions of the companies he worked for and his biggest accomplishments in each position, Jack's marketing credentials stand out. The redesign of his resume mirrors his original choice of highlighting the continuity of his employment but allows much more room for text. He has also eliminated unnecessary information under the Education section. (Typeface: Bookman)

Before

```
Jack Robertson
6889 Cranberry Road
Philadelphia, Pennsylvania 67891
(215) 555-9087 (home)
```

MARKETING EXPERIENCE

<u>10/88-present</u>	Doyle Chemical Products, Trenton, NJ As Senior Marketing Representative, I interact with Business Area Managers assisting in the planning of marketing efforts and executing all communications programs, including advertising, trade shows, and sales promotions.
<u>8/86-10/88</u>	Household Paper Manufacturers, Newark, NJ As a Marketing Specialist, I was responsible for overseeing the creative design and implementation of advertising, product promotions, sales brochures, direct mail, and field sales communications. Worked directly with Product Managers in planning and implementing new product introductions.
<u>6/81-8/86</u>	Saxon Enterprises, Princeton, NJ As Product Manager, I was responsible for all phases of product development, including determining market needs, defining product requirements, negotiating functional specifications, planning product introductions, and initiating sales support.
EDUCATION	Rutgers University, New Brunswick, NJ Bachelor of Science—May 1981 Major: Marketing—Grade Point Average 3.5
ACTIVITIES AND AWARDS	Vice President, New Jersey Regional Chapter, Association of Marketing Professionals 1990-92
	AMP Marketing Professional of the Year, 1989
INTERESTS	Fly fishing, reading political thrillers, Big Brother

After

Jack Robertson
6889 Cranberry Road
Philadelphia, Pennsylvania 67891
(215) 555-9087 (home)

MARKETING EXPERIENCE

10/88–present   **Senior Marketing Representative,** Doyle Chemical
Products, Trenton, NJ ($2.5-billion chemical
manufacturer)
—Have contributed to overall company profit
increases averaging 15 percent a year for three
years (10 percent higher than five years
preceding my tenure)
—Work with five division heads to formulate
marketing strategies for each product area, a
teamwork approach I introduced
—Instituted new product promotions with
customers, which included samples, an
innovation that prompted increased orders
and compliments from customers

8/86–10/88   **Marketing Specialist,** Household Paper
Manufacturers, Newark, NJ ($250-million paper
product manufacturer)
• Introduced new paper-towel line, which has
captured a 5 percent market share since its
inception
• Oversaw design and implementation of
advertising, product promotions, sales
brochures, direct mail, and field sales
communications for twenty-five products
• Conducted research that convinced senior
management to reposition three products, all
of which saw sales increases of 5–10 percent
in 1988

6/81–8/86   **Product Manager,** Saxon Enterprises, Princeton,
NJ ($100-million photo supplies manufacturer)
• Helped launch darkroom products division by
surveying market needs, defining product
requirements, and negotiating product
specifications
• Worked with marketing and sales department to
sell new line, which accounted for 10 percent
of company's profits after three years

EDUCATION   B.S., Rutgers University, May 1981

ACTIVITIES
AND AWARDS   Vice President, New Jersey Regional Chapter,
Association of Marketing Professionals, 1990–92
AMP Marketing Professional of the Year, 1989

INTERESTS   Fly fishing, reading political thrillers, Big Brother
program

Chronological Format

Changing Careers

John has been working as a coach and athletic director since playing basketball during college. He recently earned an M.B.A. and would like to change career paths and combine his interest in sports with his business training.

ANALYSIS

John's "before" resume is amateurish. It does not reflect the resume writer's marketing background. The job tasks sound as if they have been lifted from a personnel manual; several are repeated under two similar jobs. No attention is given to results or accomplishments.

John's revised resume is a much better marketing piece because he has chosen to emphasize those aspects of his current job that an employer from the business world can understand—how his efforts resulted in increased motivation, better attendance, and increased revenue. (Typeface: Times)

Before

John Jacobson   44 Wittenberg Road   Oxford, Ohio 43590

_____(513) 555-0987 (h)_____(513) 555-9000 (w)_____

Job Objective: A position in sports management

Education: 1992, M.B.A., Miami University
            1978, B.S., Marketing, Michigan State
            University

Work Experience:

Miami University, Oxford, Ohio
DIRECTOR OF INTERCOLLEGIATE ATHLETICS, 1986-present
-- Responsible for operation of entire athletic program
-- Prepare annual athletic and student activities budgets
-- Hire, evaluate, and supervise coaches and intramural
   staff
-- Determine eligibility in accordance with NJCAA
   regulations
-- Arrange payroll disbursements for staff
-- Purchase uniforms, equipment, and supplies
-- Schedule maintenance of fields, gym set-ups, clean-ups
-- Promote and monitor all campus athletic events and
   activities
-- Market athletic program

Baldwin-Wallace College, Berea, Ohio
ASSISTANT DIRECTOR OF INTERCOLLEGIATE ATHLETICS,
   1982-1986
-- Assisted director in operation of entire athletic
   program
-- Helped hire and supervise coaches and intramural staff
-- Purchased uniforms, equipment, and supplies
-- Scheduled maintenance of fields, gym set-ups,
   clean-ups
-- Acted as head coach for basketball team

University of Toledo, Toledo, Ohio
HEAD BASKETBALL COACH, 1978-1982
-- Recruited promising high school players for team
-- Led team through four winning seasons
-- Arranged conference schedules

Personal Sports Involvement:
Forward, Michigan State University Spartans, 1976-1978
Cyclist (changed sports after 1978 knee injury); have
   participated in 100 cycling events in last fourteen
   years

After

John Jacobson

44 Wittenberg Road   (513) 555-0987 (h)
Oxford, Ohio 43590   (513) 555-9000 (w)

Job Objective   A marketing position with a sporting goods manufacturer

Education   1992, M.B.A., Miami University
                1978, B.S., Marketing, Michigan State University

Work   **Miami University,** Oxford, Ohio, 1986–present
Experience   Director of Intercollegiate Athletics
                • Direct athletic program, which produced annual
                    revenues of $2-million and operated on a $1-million
                    budget
                • Supervise twenty-five-member intramural coaching
                    staff who have collectively improved their team's
                    win/loss records by 25 percent
                • Improved attendance at intramural events by 20 percent
                    to highest levels in school's history in 1991–92
                    school year
                • Played a major role in launching new $3-million
                    intramural sports facility

                Baldwin-Wallace College, Berea, Ohio, 1982–1986
                Assistant Director of Intercollegiate Activities
                • Helped coordinate an athletic program that featured
                    three intramural teams and twenty-five intramural
                    programs
                • Evaluated and made hiring recommendations for three
                    coaching positions
                • Purchased uniforms, equipment, and supplies
                • Scheduled maintenance of fields, gym set-ups,
                    clean-ups
                • Determined player eligibility

                University of Toledo, Toledo, Ohio, 1978–1982
                Head Basketball Coach
                • Recruited players with academic and sports potential
                • Led team through four winning seasons

Personal   Forward, Michigan State University Spartans, 1976–1978
Sports   Cyclist (changed sports after 1978 knee injury); have
Involvement   participated in 100 cycling events in last fourteen years

---

Functional Format

Changing Careers

Marie Jonello has been working as a social worker and administrator of social services for twenty years. To supplement her income in the last five years, she has worked part-time as a real estate broker. She hopes to change careers and find a job in private industry as a relocation counselor for a large company.

ANALYSIS

Except for the job objective, Marie's "before" resume does not effectively communicate why she is a good candidate for this career move. There are too many details about her social work career and not enough analysis of transferable skills and experiences.

In her revised resume, Marie has made a persuasive argument for her career change in her Summary of Qualifications. She supports it further with a functional resume whose areas of expertise parallel the experience necessary for success as a relocation counselor. (Typeface: Optima)

Before

MARIE JONELLO

19 Webster Road, N. Miami, Florida, 33138   (305) 555-9875

OBJECTIVE

A position as a relocation counselor

REAL ESTATE EXPERIENCE

Real estate agent, Century 21, Fort Lauderdale, Florida,
1987-present
Handled residential real estate sales. Put in 10 hours a week in
floor time. Developed client lists. Worked with relocation
services of major companies. Sold an average of $1-million worth
of homes annually. Built database of 500 clients.

SOCIAL WORK EXPERIENCE

Director, Rosemont Rehabilitation Center, Fort Lauderdale,
Florida, 1985-present
Total responsibility for this 100-bed, inpatient treatment
facility for substance abusers. Hired and supervised professional
staff of twenty and twenty-five hourly employees. Devised and
directed therapy programs. Personally led five sessions per week.
Acted on recommendations of intake counselors; average of five
new patients admitted weekly. Introduced posttreatment tracking
systems to determine treatment effectiveness. Two-year follow-up
showed that 50 percent of patients were active in AA and employed
one year after graduating from our program.
Substance abuse counselor, The Lakeland Institute, Lorain, Ohio,
1982-85
Evaluated average of fifteen patients per week and made
recommendations on intake. Worked with adult and juvenile
patients. Counseled families on how to perform crisis
interventions. Successfully coached over 100 families through
intervention process. Worked one-on-one and in group counseling
sessions with patients. Counseled family members on how to help
their loved one after treatment.
Resident Advisor, Evergreen Home for Girls, Lexington, Kentucky,
1977-82
Supervised twenty delinquent adolescent girls in residential
setting. Enforced disciplinary code. Counseled residents
one-on-one for emotional, psychological, and substance abuse
problems. Encouraged girls to excel in their studies; helped with
homework.
Social Worker, City of Pittsburgh, 1972-77
Supervised a caseload of fifty families. Evaluated living
situation and family life to determine appropriate action; made
recommendations to supervisory board. Advised clients on range of
services available, including special education programs, housing
applications, substance abuse treatment programs, disability, and
food stamp and welfare benefits.

EDUCATION AND LICENSES

Licensed real estate salesperson, State of Florida, 1987
Real Estate Certificate Program, Dade Community College, 1987
Master's in Social Work, Columbia University, 1972
B.A., English, Hunter College, 1970

After

MARIE JONELLO

19 Webster Road   N. Miami, Florida 33138   (305) 555-9875

SUMMARY OF QUALIFICATIONS As a counseling professional with twenty years of experience and a real estate broker with five years' experience, I can anticipate problems and offer practical housing, education, and other solutions for families being relocated by their company. Having made five major moves in my adult life, I am sensitive to the adjustments that relocation requires and how to make transitions smoother.

REAL ESTATE
- Averaged $1-million in residential real estate sales a year for past four years selling part-time
- Specialized in working with relocation services of major companies; successfully placed twenty clients in last two years
- Have demonstrated a capacity to work with the most difficult and demanding clients, who were referred to me by my office manager because of my ability to handle them

COUNSELING
- Evaluated clients' problems and concerns by asking questions, listening carefully to answers and comparing information gathered from close friends, relatives, and employers
- Worked one-on-one and in a group setting to make clients aware of their behavior and its effect on their work, families, and personal life
- Received 50 letters from substance abusers in recovery who credit me with playing a major role in their return to sobriety

ADMINISTRATION
- Orchestrated the successful functioning of a facility employing fifty-five people and treating as many as 100 clients at a time; follow-up surveys indicate program success—50 percent of clients sober and working a year after their "graduation"
- Built a database of 500 clients on computer; by maintaining regular contact, successfully did business with one third

EMPLOYMENT HISTORY
Real Estate Agent, Century 21, Fort Lauderdale, Florida, 1987–present
Director, Rosemont Rehabilitation Center, Fort Lauderdale, Florida, 1985–present
Substance Abuse Counselor, The Lakeland Institute, Lorain, Ohio, 1982–85
Resident Advisor, Evergreen Home for Girls, Lexington, Kentucky, 1977–82
Social Worker, City of Pittsburgh, 1972–77

EDUCATION AND LICENSES
Licensed real estate salesperson, State of Florida, 1987
Real Estate Certificate Program, Dade Community College, 1987
Master's in Social Work, Columbia University, 1972
B.A., English, Hunter College, 1970

INTERESTS
Deep-sea fishing, underwater photography, bridge

Combination Chronological/ Functional Format

Changing Careers

Sheryl Jamison has been a writer and editor for twenty years and has occasionally taught writing courses. She now wants to change careers and move into a full-time faculty position at a university.

ANALYSIS

Sheryl's resume doesn't do her career justice. She doesn't use numbers or provide enough details in her job task descriptions. She's trying to reposition herself but that's not accomplished by using the heading "Curriculum Vitae," which is commonly seen on academic resumes. Instead, she needs to emphasize the skills she has developed as a reporter and editor that would help her candidacy as a would-be professor.

Sheryl revised her resume into a two-page combination chronological/functional format. It works well for her because it gives her the space to expand on her teaching and journalism skills in the Areas of Expertise section. By including a job objective and positioning her teaching experience before her journalism work history at the top, Sheryl makes it clear right from the start what she wants to do and why she is qualified to do it. (Typeface: New Century Schoolbook)

Before

```
                    Curriculum Vitae
                     Sheryl Jamison
26 West 75th Street                    (212) 555-9823 (h)
New York, NY 10023                     (212) 555-9000 (w)
                       EXPERIENCE
```

Crain's New York Business, 1982–present

Senior editor, 1989–present
- Generate, assign, and edit one third of this business weekly
- Write occasional full-length features, particularly profile pieces
- Oversee work of contributing editors and free-lance staff
- Coordinate editorial with design staff and serve as a liaison with production and research departments

Editor, Media Department, 1982–1989
- Covered the media beat and wrote more than fifty news stories and features
- Covered the real estate beat and wrote more than thirty-five news stories, features, and a weekly real estate wrap-up
- Interviewed top business people, including magazine publishers and editors, book publishers and editors, owners of media conglomerates, and Wall Street media analysts

Business Week, 1972–1982

Staff editor, 1977–1982
- Reported and edited stories with an emphasis on major economic trends, corporate marketing strategies, and advertising news. Originated story ideas and worked closely with domestic and international bureaus.

Reporter, 1972–1977
- Developed story ideas for company profiles and trend stories; wrote fifteen cover stories and ten major inside features
- Won Overseas Press Club young reporter award for series on impact of student demonstrations on business

TEACHING
New York University School of Journalism
Adjunct Professor, 1985–present
- Teach news and feature writing courses to undergraduates (one per year); earned "10" rating in student evaluations, the highest possible rating

EDUCATION
M.A., Columbia School of Journalism, 1972
B.A., Pennsylvania State University, 1971

INTERESTS
Karate (have earned brown belt), playing folk guitar, reading mystery novels

After

Sheryl Jamison

26 West 75th Street   (212) 555-9823 (h)
New York, NY 10023   (212) 555-9000 (w)

JOB OBJECTIVE
A full-time faculty position within the journalism department of a
university

EXPERIENCE
New York University School of Journalism
Adjunct Professor, 1985–present
- Teach news and feature writing courses to undergraduates (one per
  year)

Crain's New York Business, 1982–present
Senior editor, 1989–present
- Generate, assign, and edit one third of this business weekly
- Oversee work of contributing editors and free-lance staff

Editor, Media Department, 1982–1989
- Covered the media beat and wrote more than fifty news stories and
  features
- Covered the real estate beat and wrote more than thirty-five stories
  and a weekly wrap-up

Business Week, 1972–1982
Staff editor, 1977–1982
- Reported and edited stories with an emphasis on major economic
  trends, corporate marketing strategies, and advertising news
- Originated story ideas and worked closely with domestic and
  international bureaus

Reporter, 1972–1977
- Developed ideas for company profiles and trend stories; wrote fifteen
  cover stories and ten major inside features, one of which won
  Overseas Press Club Award (1977)

EDUCATION
M.A., Columbia School of Journalism, 1972
B.A., Pennsylvania State University, 1971

INTERESTS
Karate (have earned brown belt); playing folk guitar; reading mystery
novels

(continued)

Sheryl Jamison

26 West 75th Street   (212) 555-9823 (h)
New York, NY 10023   (212) 555-9000 (w)

AREAS OF EXPERTISE

Teaching
- Taught news and feature writing courses to undergraduates (one per year)
- Earned "10" rating in student evaluations, the highest possible rating
- Developed and moderated two of ten special panels for journalism faculty and students during 1991–92 school year

Editing and Writing
- Developed story ideas, conducted research, wrote story proposals
- Interviewed business leaders, Wall Street analysts, economists, company presidents, and government officials
- Have written more than 200 business trend stories, profiles, and features

Communication
- Edited stories of top business writers and columnists, with whom I developed friendly and productive working relationships
- Volunteered to work as journalism department ombudsman to resolve student-faculty disagreements
- Coordinate editorial with design staff and serve as a liaison with production and research departments

---

We'd Like to Hear from You

If *The Advanced 90-Minute Resume* has helped you, you can help us. The best way to ensure that the 90-minute process continues to work is to hear the comments and suggestions of those who have put it to use.

- What features were most helpful in revising your resume?

- Did you receive comments from employers, agencies, or others about your resume?

- Is there anything in particular about the 90-minute process that you feel could be improved?

- Do you have suggestions for what you'd like to see added or changed in a future edition?

- Would you find a computerized version of *The Advanced 90-Minute Resume* helpful? If yes, please indicate the type of personal computer you would use.

"Before" and "after" versions of your resume will also be helpful for future editions of the book. Please send your correspondence to: Peggy Schmidt, *The Advanced 90-Minute Resume,* c/o Peterson's Guides, Inc., P.O. Box 2123, Princeton, NJ 08543-2123.

About the Author

Peggy Schmidt writes "Your New Job," a nationally syndicated weekly newspaper column, and is the author of *The 90-Minute Resume*, for job hunters who are writing their resume for the first time, and *Making It on Your First Job*. She has also been a career columnist for *Glamour* and *New Woman* magazines. As career coordinator for the New York University Summer Publishing Institute, Schmidt has given resume tips and job hunting advice to hundreds of individuals.